Handmade in America

THE HERITAGE OF COLONIAL CRAFTSMEN

BOOKS BY SIGMUND A. LAVINE

Famous Merchants

Famous Industrialists

Kettering: Master Inventor

Steinmetz, Maker of Lightning

Allan Pinkerton, America's First Private Eye

Wonders of the Anthill

Wonders of the Hive

Wonders of the Wasp's Nest

Wonders of the Beetle World

Wonders of Animal Disguises

Wonders of Animal Architecture

Strange Partners

Strange Travelers

Water Since the World Began, *with Mart Casey*

Handmade in America

THE HERITAGE OF COLONIAL CRAFTSMEN

by Sigmund A. Lavine
ILLUSTRATED WITH PHOTOGRAPHS

DODD, MEAD & COMPANY · NEW YORK

PICTURE CREDITS

Photographs courtesy of:

Bowdoin College Museum of Art, 16 (left)
E. F. Christman, 57 (middle)
V. G. Christman, 57 (left)
Collins Clock Museum, N.H., 55 (right), 58
The Corning Museum of Glass, 60, 72
Essex Institute, 2 (middle), 4
The Henry Ford Museum, 15 (left), 48 (top), 82 (middle), 110 (left), 118 (right)
Hitchcock Chair Company, 30, 31, 32, 33, 34
Patrick Kelley, 9
Lenox, 86, 87
The Mariners Museum, Newport News, Va., 6
The Metropolitan Museum of Art, Rogers Fund, 1922, 27
The Metropolitan Museum of Art, Gift of Mr. and Mrs. Lowell Ross Burch and Miss Jean
    McLean Marron, 1951, 35 (top)
Museum of Fine Arts, Boston, 99 (top)
New Orleans Chamber of Commerce, 121 (top)
Norcross, Inc., 132, 134
Old Sturbridge Village, 2 (top & bottom), 11, 43 (right), 48 (bottom left), 52 (left), 65 (top),
    66 (left), 80, 82 (top right), 101, 102 (top), 105, 108 (bottom), 116, 117, 124, 125, 127, 128
    (top), 131
Parke-Bernet Galleries, 8, 10, 14, 15 (right), 16 (top & right), 17 (bottom), 18, 19, 20, 21, 22, 23,
    26, 29, 35 (middle), 37, 38, 39, 40, 41, 43 (left), 48 (bottom right), 54 (right), 61, 62,
    63, 65 (middle), 66 (right), 68, 70, 73 (left), 75, 82 (bottom), 90, 111, 122 (bottom)
Revere Copper and Brass, Inc., 97 (right), 110 (right), 112 (left), 114 (top)
The Smithsonian Institution, 45 (right), 82 (top left), 129
Steuben Glass, 77
Vernon Stoneman, 24
Towle Silversmiths, 89, 91, 92 (top & middle left & right), 94, 99 (left)
Dr. Harry E. Trapp, 128 (bottom)
Trefry-Partridge, 92 (bottom), 96
United States Army Photograph, 119
University of Pennsylvania, 46
Weiner's Antique Shop, Boston, 17 (top left & right), 28, 35 (bottom), 45 (left), 52 (middle &
    right), 54 (middle), 55 (left & middle), 57 (right), 65 (bottom), 73 right, 76, 84, 97 (left),
    102 (bottom), 108 (top), 112 (right), 122 (top), 135

Library of Congress Catalog Card Number: 66-13347

Printed in the United States of America

For Hyman Weiner:

IN GRATITUDE FOR KNOWLEDGE SHARED
AND FRIENDSHIP ENJOYED

Acknowledgments

While dozens of people—museum curators, antique dealers, private collectors, authors of reference works, and experts in the field of economic history—have aided in the writing of this book, the greatest contributions were made by Hyman Weiner and Rosemary Casey.

It was "Hy" who taught me to recognize and appreciate the work of skilled craftsmen as we sat talking in his famous antique shop directly across the street from historic Boston Common in the shadow of the golden dome of the Massachusetts' State House. Often while calling my attention to a detail seen only with a trained eye, he would express the hope that someday I would "put this all in a book." The chances are I never would have done so without the encouragement of Rosemary Casey of Dodd, Mead & Company, who not only aided me in the undertaking, but also assumed the task of preparing my manuscript for publication. I am grateful to them both.

Special thanks are also due to Louise Bonar, of the book department of the Boston *Herald*; Lee Collins, curator of Collins Clock Museum, Georges Mills, New Hampshire; James J. Keeney, director of public relations, Old Sturbridge Village, Sturbridge, Massachusetts; Reverend Louis Ketron, Mountain View Methodist Church, Dayton, Tennessee; Isobel C. Lee, vice-president, Steuben Glass Company, New York City; Jane Lanahan, registrar of the Corning Museum of Glass, Corning, New York; Esther B. Mooney, curator of the Norcross Greeting Card Collection, New York City; Revere Copper and Brass Company, New York City; Linda Rosenkrantz, publicity department, Parke-Bernet Galleries, New York City; Forrest Seymour, editor, Worcester *Telegram*; Vernon Stoneman, antiquarian, Boston, Massachusetts; Elizabeth Swan, State Street Bank and Trust Company, Boston, Massachusetts; Towle Silversmiths, Newburyport, Massachusetts; Paul Weiner, Weiner's Antique Shop, Boston, Massachusetts; and the library staff of the Boston Museum of Fine Arts who allowed me to work in the stacks.

Finally, I must express my appreciation to the staff of the Public Library of Milton, Massachusetts, and to the "day-side" crew of the library of the Boston *Herald*. As always, despite my demands on their time, energy, and patience, they have been most gracious and helpful.

Contents

INTRODUCTION   I

1   WORKERS IN WOOD   3

2   CABINETMAKERS   13

3   CLOCKMAKERS   42

4   GLASSMAKERS   59

5   PORCELAIN AND POTTERY MAKERS   79

6   WORKERS IN PRECIOUS METALS   88

7   PEWTERERS   100

8   WORKERS IN BASE METALS   107

9   PATCH, PASTE, AND PEN CRAFTS   126

BIBLIOGRAPHY   137

INDEX   140

Handmade in America
THE HERITAGE OF COLONIAL CRAFTSMEN

Introduction

"... the craft so long to lerne ..."
—CHAUCER

Firm in their faith in God and convinced that they could sustain them-selves with gun, ax, and plow, the more daring among Europe's oppressed set sail for the New World in the seventeenth century. Despite epidemics, natural disasters, and raids by hostile Indians, most of their settlements eventually became thriving communities. During this period of growth, no group was more important than those who had the skill to work wood, mold metals, blow glass, or build houses and make the furnishings for them.

This is the story of these individuals, their working methods, their products, and how they trained others to carry on the ancient traditions of the craftsman. Hampered at times by a lack of raw materials, at others by restrictive laws, these artisans borrowed the best from the past while developing techniques and styles that were typically American. From their shops came not only useful articles but also decorative objects, beautifully designed and richly ornamented.

While several of the men whose careers are described on these pages are well known in other fields, most have no claim to fame except their skill. But all played an important part in the economic growth of this country. Each craft has been treated separately in the chapters that follow, their order being in no way an evaluation of their relative importance before complex machinery replaced hand tools and sprawling factories began to mass produce wares once painstakingly fashioned by individuals.

ABOVE: *Crude wooden knife box or tray made in the early 19th century. Approximately 8" x 12½". Painted dark gray and decorated with black brush strokes and dots.*

RIGHT: *Medallion head of George Washington carved by Samuel McIntire, from Salem Common (Washington Square), now in the Essex Institute, Salem, Massachusetts.*

BELOW: *To catch the eye of shoppers, craftsmen hung signs above their shops that depicted their wares. A New England bootery.*

I

Workers in Wood

————————————————

The art of wood carving began as a necessity in America and developed into an art. Because of the lack of other materials, early settlers were forced to make tools and utensils out of wood. At first, these articles were whittled with a knife, but when pioneer craftsmen set up their primitive shops most of them were fashioned on a lathe—a machine which holds an object and rotates it while it is being shaped by a tool.

However, even after Massachusetts-born Thomas Blanchard designed a lathe which could turn irregular shapes—an innovation that made possible mass production of gunstocks, shoe lasts, oblong and square woodenware —craftsmen who could use knife and chisel skillfully were still in demand. Some found ready employment in shops of cabinetmakers and chair-makers, while others carved decoys (imitations of wild fowl). Still others specialized in creating shop signs, ship figureheads, or in decorating interior woodwork. A few even accepted commissions to make busts of prominent citizens.

The inscription on the stone above the grave of Samuel McIntire in Salem, Massachusetts, informs the reader that McIntire was "Distinguished for Genius in Architecture, Sculpture, and Musick" but does not mention his carving skill. Yet McIntire was the outstanding practitioner of wood carving during the late eighteenth century and is famous both for his intricately carved furniture—rated as among the finest ever made in this country—and his ornamentation of interior woodwork.

McIntire was born in Salem in 1757. His father was a joiner and, after teaching his son that craft, apprenticed him to a master carver. While little is known of McIntire's early life, it is safe to assume that he carved figure-heads as a journeyman in a Salem shipyard. The city was then one of the busiest ports on the eastern seaboard and became known to sailors as the "Pepper Box" because all the pepper imported from the East Indies was discharged there.

After marrying Elizabeth Field in 1778, McIntire opened a large wood-working shop behind his home. Here he made furniture and did carving for the Sandersons, exporters of furniture to the southern states, East and West Indies, and South America. When not busy in his shop, McIntire spent his time reading or relaxing by playing the double bass, the violin, or his "large hand organ with ten barrels." His library was that of a scholar, including volumes dealing with art, architecture, sculpture, music, and science.

In 1782, McIntire began designing and building houses in Salem and, in addition, decorated their interiors and fashioned furniture for them. While his brothers did the carpentry work, McIntire carved the doorways, mantels, and the interior trim. He used the same designs on woodwork as he did on furniture: sheaves of wheat, rosettes, eagles, grape clusters, overflowing cornucopias, urns filled with flowers, and baskets of fruit.

McIntire's buildings were among the most beautiful of those built in New England during the Federal Period. Fortunately, many still stand, enabling us to see the work in its entirety. As he grew older, McIntire was assisted by his son, Samuel Field McIntire, who, while lacking his father's genius, was nevertheless an excellent craftsman.

In 1792, McIntire entered the first public architectural competition held in America by submitting a design for the proposed Capitol Building in

Doorway of Pingree House, 128 Essex Street, Salem, Massachusetts, carved by Samuel McIntire in 1804.

Washington, but his plan was rejected. However, he did get commissions to erect several public buildings in Salem, all of which he decorated in his characteristic style. When the Salem Common was laid out and named Washington Square, McIntire created wooden gateways—elaborate arches ornamented with carvings—for the east and west entrances. The western arch contained a medallion likeness of Washington nearly fifteen feet square, carved from sketches McIntire had made of Washington when he visited Salem in 1789.

Few of McIntire's sculptures have been located. The best known one is the bust of Governor John Winthrop of Massachusetts, commissioned by the Reverend William Bentley. Although the Reverend did not approve of the bust at first, he later changed his mind and, when McIntire died on February 6, 1811, Bentley wrote, "This day Salem was deprived of one of the most ingenious men it had in it."

McIntire was ingenious and talented, and a master carver. Yet he died a relatively poor man. However, his son inherited complete sets of joiner's, carver's, and draughting tools, "including three hundred chisels and gouges and forty-six molding planes"—perhaps the largest assortment of tools owned by any craftsman of the period.

When primitive man had first ventured onto the open sea, he often painted an eye or a fearsome beast on the prow of his ship. The eye was to enable the vessel to find its way; the beast to frighten foes. These superstitions led to the placing of figureheads on ships. In time, it became the custom to adorn a vessel with a figurehead which symbolized her name, or with one that appealed to the artistic taste of her owner. As a rule, figureheads were carved by trained sculptors who were also called upon to display their skill on the stern and other parts of a vessel. By the end of the eighteenth century so much carved wood was used to decorate ships—even the cannon portholes of men-of-war were surrounded by carved wreaths—that its weight made the ships top-heavy and difficult to maneuver.

Gradually, the excessive load of carvings was eliminated, but figureheads were retained. However, although a small number were executed by trained artists, the majority were carved by artisans who had learned their craft as apprentices or by individuals with a natural talent. Such men are called folk artists.

The outstanding figurehead carvers in America were William Rush (1756-1833) of Philadelphia, who also made the wooden statue of Washington in Independence Hall; John Haley Bellamy (1836-1914), who specialized in work for the United States Navy in his shop at Kittery, Maine (his best known work is the tremendous eagle with a wingspread of eighteen feet originally made for the *U.S. Lancaster*, now displayed at the

LEFT: *Neptune, mythical god of the sea, made a majestic figurehead as can be seen from this picture. To the right of Neptune is the carving of a sea serpent which once decorated a sailing vessel.* RIGHT: *Figurehead from the bark* Belle of Oregon *built in 1876 at Bath, Maine.*

Once the figurehead of the U.S. Navy steam frigate Lancaster, *this wooden eagle, with a wing-spread of over eighteen feet, was carved by John Haley Bellamy of Kittery Point, Maine, in the 1880's when the* Lancaster *was rebuilt at the Portsmouth, New Hampshire, Navy Yard.*

Marine Museum in Portsmouth, Virginia); and the Skillin family of Boston.

Eldest of the Skillins was Simeon, Sr., (1716-1778), who taught his sons, Samuel, James, John, and Simeon, Jr., to carve. While Simeon, Sr., was an extremely competent carver—about 1775 he fashioned a bust of Milton, the English poet, out of a block of solid mahogany—three of his sons, John, Samuel, and Simeon, Jr., had equal skill.

Samuel, who operated a shop for a short time in Philadelphia, not only carved the bust of Benjamin Franklin now in the Franklin Institute but also did the carving on the vessels in the Pennsylvania Navy during the Revolution. Upon his return to Boston, Samuel was commissioned to make the first figurehead for the *U.S. Constitution*, receiving $719.33 for his work. His name appears in the Boston directory in 1796, so it is very likely he helped his brothers John and Simeon, Jr., in 1795 when Charles Bulfinch, the famous architect, gave them a commission to carve the eighteen Corinthian columns for the new Massachusetts State House which Bulfinch was constructing on the top of Beacon Hill, where signal fires had once burned to guide ships into Boston Harbor.

Besides carving figureheads and ornamenting woodwork, John Skillin made furniture at "Mess'rs Skillins' Carver's Shop Near Governor Hancock's Wharf." He worked in collaboration with his brother Simeon, and their carving has so much in common that it is nearly impossible to credit either one with a specific figurehead or any of the ornamental figures made by the Skillins to embellish the fronts of buildings or for use as garden decorations. After John's death in 1800, Simeon, Jr., continued to operate the family shop and "not only did he carve figureheads for ships but innumerable chairs, sideboards, desks, and other pieces of furniture."

When the custom of placing figureheads on vessels was discontinued, many carvers were thrown out of work. However, a considerable number turned to fashioning shop signs in the form of animals, boots, clocks, gloves, spectacles, mortars and pestles, and razors for tradesmen to hang above their doors. Then, suddenly, in the mid-eighteenth century, carvers who could produce human figures were again in demand—every tobacco shop wanted a "cigar-store" Indian.

From 1850, almost to the present day, a wooden Indian "identified the tobacco store as readily as the red-and-white striped pole marks the barber shop." Most of these advertising effigies were made by semiskilled carvers who worked in large shops. The making and selling of cigar-store Indians was a well-organized business and, according to one authority, salesmen showed prospective customers illustrated price lists and offered them discounts on such items as "extra special Pocahontases." The large establishment of S. A. Robb in New York City accepted "trade-ins" on the latest

LEFT: *Like hundreds of other hand-carved and painted wooden Indians, this figure once marked the location of a shop where tobacco was sold.* RIGHT: *While most tobacco dealers placed a "cigar-store Indian" in front of their shops, some preferred other emblems. Among the most popular of these was a female figure in Turkish dress. This one has a red turban, green dress, and red shoes.*

models and also repaired and repainted old figures. The price of the average wooden Indian ranged from fifty to one hundred dollars, while those carved by such well-known sculptors as Julius Theodore Melchers of Detroit and Herman Matzen of Cleveland were considerably higher.

Today, most cigar-store Indians have vanished. Those that have survived and which are not displayed by tobacconists are eagerly sought by collectors as an example of folk art—and their carvers would be astonished at the prices now paid for their squaws and chiefs.

Just about the time when the demand for cigar-store Indians began to taper off, wagon builders were seeking carvers to decorate the sides of circus wagons with figures and scroll work. While a few examples of circus carvings have been preserved, practically nothing is known of the men who

LEFT: *The famous ornately carved and gilded Columbia Circus band wagon now displayed in the Circus World Museum at Baraboo, Wisconsin.* ABOVE: *Carved and gilded wooden figures taken from an early circus calliope, a musical instrument with a series of steam whistles, played like an organ.*

made them, or of their fellow craftsmen who created the animals used on carrousels. However, it is established that Samuel Robb did many carvings for Barnum and Bailey, "the greatest show on Earth," and that a man named Charles Louff excelled in carving vigorous and realistic animals for carrousels.

While professional carvers were employed in shipyards, furniture shops, cigar-store Indian manufactories, and wagon works, thousands of amateurs were engaged in whittling useful and decorative objects. During the winter, when they were unable to work outside, farmers fashioned butter molds—stamps with a handle for imprinting a pat of butter with a design. They also carved box molds which had an ornament cut in the top piece. These boxes held a pound of "print butter" which sold for a higher price than butter

9

Scrimshaw carvings show a wide range of taste. Along with other decorations, the walrus tusk on the left is covered with a bust of Washington, a peacock, several famous monuments, young ladies, and a monogram. Some music-loving sailor carved a full-length picture of Jenny Lind, the famous Swedish singer, on the whale's jawbone in the center, while a deeply religious tar pinpricked pictures of St. Peter's Church in Rome and of well-known English ministers on the right-hand walrus tusk.

dispensed in bulk. Other whittlers turned out weathervanes, decoys, or toys for their children.

Farmers were not the only whittlers. Sailors avoided boredom on long voyages by carving a wide variety of articles. It was while shipping before the mast that young Samuel Colt carved a wooden pattern of the gun which was to bring him fame and play an important part in the taming of the West.

Not all sailors worked in wood—some preferred doing scrimshaw. This consisted of carving designs and pictures on whale's teeth and then rubbing India ink into the hollows to make them black. Walrus tusks were also used in scrimshaw work and often the scratch carvings on them were tinted with colors rubbed into the lines.

Many hunters and trappers were also expert whittlers. Often they put their skill with a knife to practical use by carving a map of the region over which they roamed on the surface of their powder horns. Soldiers spent so much time and effort in carving their powder horns that a regulation was passed requiring that, in addition to any ornamentation, a soldier's powder horn should bear his name so that it could be immediately returned to him after being refilled at the powder-wagon. This rule prevented arguments over the ownership of well-carved horns.

A considerable number of lumberjacks were clever carvers, as were many migratory workers, but perhaps the most outstanding amateur carver was Dr. Robert S. Grier, a Presbyterian minister whose farm was bisected by the boundary line between Pennsylvania and Maryland. Dr. Grier carved cane heads, statuettes, and many other articles, but he is best known for his eagles.

After the War Between the States every innkeeper near Gettysburg, Pennsylvania—where the most decisive battle of that conflict was fought— wanted a Grier eagle to place over his door. However, the doctor had died in 1865 and few who owned examples of his work were willing to sell them. Therefore, all who desired an eagle ordered one from William Schimmel, a wandering workman. He made his headquarters in Carlisle, Pennsylvania, which was famous as the home of Mary Ludwig, better known as "Molly Pitcher" because she carried water in a pitcher to the colonists during the

Although factories were turning out thousands of pieces of mass-produced furniture by the mid-nineteenth century, country craftsmen continued to operate their one-man shops catering to local needs.

battle of Monmouth in 1778. But Schimmel wasn't interested in history—the only things that concerned him were a place to sleep and something to eat, and he much preferred to pay for them with a carving rather than by working in the fields.

Besides carving eagles, Schimmel fashioned parrots and various animals. While Dr. Grier's eagles show great technical skill, those made by Schimmel are vigorous but far cruder. Like his handiwork, Schimmel was rough and on one occasion when his carvings failed to win a prize at a fair he flew into a violent rage which added to his reputation for being unpleasant. Yet he was always willing to carve a toy for a child. Nevertheless, when he died, a penniless vagrant in a poorhouse in 1890, a newspaper report of his death noted ". . . old Schimmel was apparently a man of surly disposition."

Although men continued to whittle for pleasure, factory-made articles eventually replaced homemade wooden ones, just as the mass production of furniture ended the era of the master carvers who worked in the cabinet-making shops of large cities. However, the craft of wood carving was revived in Cincinnati, Ohio, in the mid-nineteenth century by English-born Henry H. Fry, who had studied under such outstanding craftsmen as Sir Charles Barry, who not only designed Westminster Palace but also the furniture used in its many rooms. Fry, himself, was commissioned to carve the throne chair for Queen Victoria before coming to Cincinnati with his son, William H. Fry (who was also a master carver), in 1851.

Both father and son did carvings for private and public buildings and both became members of the faculty of the Cincinnati Art School. In addition to working with his father, William Fry, using traditional motifs such as acanthus leaves, ornamented pianos and many smaller objects.

The Frys were responsible for making wood carving popular in Cincinnati. In 1873, Benn Pitman, the brother of Sir Isaac Pitman of England, who is not only famous for inventing a system of shorthand but also for being the first to suggest the use of postage stamps on prepaid letters, began teaching wood carving to a class of sixty women at the Cincinnati Art Academy. When not in the classroom Pitman kept busy—from 1895 to 1905—by carving the interior woodwork of his son's house, covering every bit of wooden trim with representations of flowers native to Ohio.

Like the Frys and Pitman, other individuals, despite living in the machine age, kept alive the craft of wood carving. Today, in artists' studios and exclusive shops where furniture is made to order, master craftsmen still use knife and chisel. However, it is extremely doubtful that wood carving will ever be as popular in the future as it was in Portsmouth, Ohio, in 1848. The residents of that city could boast that *every* telephone pole along its streets was topped with a carving of an animal, bird, Indian, or famous person!

2

Cabinetmakers

———————————⇒⊹⊹⊹⊹⇐———————————

Although the *Mayflower*'s hold was full when she sailed out of South-ampton, England, on August 5, 1620, there was very little furniture on board. Warned that the amount of cargo space was limited, the Pilgrims had left many of their possessions behind. As a result, most of the furniture aboard consisted of chests which served not only for storage but also as tables, benches without backs called "long forms," and jointed stools known as "short forms."

Probably there were few chairs in the cargo, for in the seventeenth century chairs were owned only by the wealthy. Large armchairs, then known as "great chairs," were so rare that they were mentioned in their owners' wills. A well-furnished house might contain only a single chair, which was reserved for the master of the household or for an honored guest. This made the chair a symbol of authority and, at meetings, the person in charge always sat in one—thus the origin of the word "chairman."

However, while the *Mayflower* brought little furniture to Plymouth, her passenger list included the name of the first trained woodworker to arrive in America. Originally hired to help repair the *Mayflower* in Southampton, he had joined the Pilgrims and, by so doing, solved one of their problems. British law required that every vessel have a cooper aboard to repair the casks in which salt meat and water were stored and to make new casks during the voyage to replace the ones being shipped out of the country.

The *Mayflower*'s cooper was one of the signers of the compact the Pilgrims drew up before landing at Plymouth and is said to have been the first ashore. Appointed a magistrate, he served in that office for fifty years, combining his legal duties with furniture making. However, he is best known today—because of Longfellow's famous poem—for proposing to Priscilla Mullens on behalf of his friend, Captain Miles Standish. America's first furniture maker was, of course, John Alden.

Alden formed a partnership with Kenlem Winslow, brother of the first governor of the "Plimouth Plantation," who, like many later colonial woodworkers, combined the trade of coffinmaking with the craft of cabinetmak-

LEFT: *As the colonies became more prosperous, cabinetmakers found a market for furniture made from native woods, particularly chairs such as this "pilgrim" painted and turned maple slat-back armchair with mushroom finials on the arm supports made in New England around 1700.* ABOVE: *An 18th century pine hutch table with a removable oval top above a seat with apron and closed sides.*

ing. While definite proof is lacking, experts attribute about twenty pieces of furniture to Alden and Winslow. In fact, the earliest piece of American furniture that can positively be identified is a carved oak chest "Cutte and Joyned" about 1680 by Nicholas Disbrowe of Hartford, Connecticut.

Because there was little demand for furniture during the early colonial period, cabinetmakers engaged in a wide variety of activities to earn a living. Disbrowe was no different. When business was slack he served as "chimney viewer" and "surveyor of the highways." Similarly, at a later date, Aaron Chapin, another Connecticut woodworker, advertised that he cleaned watches and offered for sale "cheap and good sundry Bass Viols, complete for use, Pitch Pipes, Fifes, Watches do. Seals, key chaines, &c." But few colonial craftsmen combined so many activities as did John Gaines of Portsmouth, New Hampshire. Not only did he make furniture, but he also manufactured rolling pins and hoe handles, built houses and churches, thatched roofs, did blacksmithing, cultivated a large farm, butchered hogs, and ran a general store.

However, as more people settled in the colonies and houses became larger, cabinetmakers found they could make a living by their craft. Unfortunately, the names of the majority of pre-Revolutionary furniture makers are unknown and most of their work has vanished, either being destroyed in the many fires that swept colonial America or discarded because it was no longer in style.

Because the colonists preferred furniture which could be used for more than one purpose, cabinetmakers supplied them with chairs, the backs of which could be let down to form a table, along with wooden "settles"—a settee which became a bed when its seat was unhooked and allowed to fall forward. However, chairs finally came into general use and, although many were imported from England, several types were made in America. Even upholstered chairs became common. Roger Williams who was banished from Massachusetts in 1635 because he "dyvulged dyvers newe and dangerous opinions"—such as treating the Indians fairly—had one, while Captain Kidd, the famous pirate, owned two dozen. Yet it wasn't until 1794 that upholstered chairs were advertised in New York City by James Huthwaite

LEFT: *A pine "settle" made in New England, 1775-1800. Decoration at ears and center of the base is an incised circle with an inner line and dot motif.* RIGHT: *Pine corner cabinet with dentiled cornice and keystone flanked by floral devices and a shell interior, carved by an unknown master craftsman in the late 17th century.*

Painted maple banister-back armchairs, the one on the right having baluster-turned arm supports continuing to stretched legs.

LEFT: *An outstanding example of early American craftsmanship: oak wainscot chair made and carved by Thomas Dennis of Ipswich, Massachusetts, about 1675.* RIGHT: *Painted and turned hutch table made of pine, the wood almost universally used by New England cabinetmakers for "cottage furniture."*

who announced that he was an "Upholsterer and Chair Stuffer from London."

Thomas Dennis of Ipswich, Massachusetts, did not advertise. Born in England in the late 1630's, he served his apprenticeship there and came to

America where his well-proportioned furniture, expertly turned and ornately decorated, found a ready market. Dennis was fond of using a band of "S" scrolls as well as formal motifs to decorate his handiwork and was the only American cabinetmaker to use a wooden cleat pin hinge on a chest —a wooden pin passed through the hole of the cleat at each end of the lid. Perhaps his most famous work is the elaborately carved oak chair used by the president of Bowdoin College, in Brunswick, Maine.

As the colonies became more prosperous, increasing numbers of English-trained master cabinetmakers came to the New World to cater to those who had accumulated fortunes in trade, shipping, fishing, and whaling. A few settled in the South, usually taking a post on a plantation where they made and repaired furniture for one family, as did the craftsman William Penn sent from England to work on his Pennsylvania estate. Others wandered about carrying the techniques of their craft from one colony to another. Still others opened shops in such thriving seaport towns as Boston and Salem, Massachusetts. While these men followed English designs—which were to dominate American furniture-making for two centuries—they varied them and gave them an individuality of their own.

Most of the furniture of the early colonial period was made in New England. As the years passed, cabinetmakers in this region not only supplied

LEFT: *By 1800, Salem, Massachusetts, was the most prosperous city of its size in America, and local cabinetmakers found a ready market for fine furniture like this side chair.* RIGHT: *Washstand made by William Hook (or Hoock), a Salem cabinetmaker whose work was "so much in demand that orders were placed sometimes a year in advance."*

William and Mary furniture— named for the Dutch prince who became king of England and his English bride—was often painted to brighten the interiors of colonial homes as was this carved, Spanish-footed day bed. The cushion is linsey-woolsey, a coarsely woven fabric.

the local demand but also sold their product to distant customers. Loaded on vessels, furniture was carried as "venture cargo" to southern ports and to the West Indies, ship captains disposing of it at the highest possible price in return for a commission. However, certain cabinetmakers had all they could do to satisfy nearby clients and left the making of furniture for export to others.

Among these was John Cogswell of Boston. The date and place of his birth are unknown, but he was well established by 1789 and proudly labeled his handiwork "Made by John Cogswell in middle Street, Boston." Cogswell had good reason to be proud for he produced the finest bombé (kettle-shaped) furniture ever made in this country. It is no easy task to bend a solid plank of mahogany to this shape, but Cogswell accomplished it skillfully.

While Cogswell and others were creating masterpieces in their individual styles, a cabinetmaker's co-operative was operating in the bustling town of Newport, Rhode Island. Located at the mouth of Narragansett Bay, Newport was a shipbuilding and fishing center as well as the home port for privateers and for vessels engaged in the slave trade. Its wealthy residents could afford the best in furniture, and it was made for them by the members of the Goddard and Townsend families.

The Goddards and Townsends were closely related by marriage, business dealings, and religion—both groups being Quakers. During the eighteenth and early nineteenth centuries, thirteen Townsends and seven Goddards, following the styles popular at the time, produced outstanding furniture. Sometimes they worked alone, but often collaborated, and it was their combined skills which created the first block-front, shell-carved furniture made in America. The purpose of blocking is to break up flat surfaces on furniture and consists of cutting the front of a piece so that there is a raised surface at either end and a depressed surface in the middle. Newport

While block-front furniture was made throughout the United States in the eighteenth century, the finest examples are the work of such New England craftsmen as the one who fashioned this carved Chippendale cherrywood block-front chest of drawers with claw and ball feet.

LEFT: *The graceful reverse scroll arms ending in scrolled terminals testify to the Philadelphia origin of this 18th century Queen Anne shell-carved walnut drake-foot armchair.* RIGHT: *Believed to have been made in 1765, this Chippendale chair exemplifies the skill of Philadelphia cabinetmakers.*

craftsmen usually cut the raised block panels on drawers and doors from a single block of wood, but occasionally cut the blocks separately, then glued them in place.

Generally, the convex shells at the top of the block were cut from the block itself—not a simple task as a single mistake would have ruined the entire piece—but sometimes these ornaments were applied. However, the concave shells at the top or bottom of the sunken central section were rarely appliquéd. Although the shells of Goddard-Townsend, block-front furniture vary in design, they appear to have been carved by one person. He was probably James Townsend, son of Job Townsend, who, with his brother Christopher, and John Goddard, were the group's leaders.

Out of the Townsend-Goddard shops where fathers passed to their sons the traditions, techniques, and secrets of the craft of cabinetmaking came furniture that was nearly flawless. Some experts rank it as the best examples of American-made furniture. But others hold that this honor belongs to the craftsmen who worked in Philadelphia during the eighteenth century.

Penn's city had become a teeming trading center and over one hundred chair and cabinet makers were established there by 1722. Within a short time the furniture craftsmen of Philadelphia were famous because "the work they produced in the Chippendale style has never been surpassed in America in beauty of design and richness of carving."

Thomas Chippendale, an English cabinetmaker, had published *The Cabinet Maker's Directory* in 1754, and it had a tremendous influence on American furniture design, as did *The Cabinet-Maker and Upholsterer's Drawing Book* published between 1792-1795, The last named was the work of Thomas Sheraton, an Englishman who never made furniture but who is credited with originating the twin bed.

Using these two books as guides, but developing individual styles, Philadelphia cabinetmakers not only supplied furniture to local customers but also to clients in New York City and the South. While a considerable amount of their production has been identified, not a great deal is known about their personal lives.

However, we do know that Thomas Affleck, who is recognized as making the finest furniture in Philadelphia Chippendale style, was arrested as a Tory in 1797 and banished to Virginia for seven months. On the other hand, Benjamin Randolph was a loyal patriot. One of the greatest of American cabinetmakers, Randolph manufactured buttons as a sideline, fashion-

BELOW: *Chippendale-carved cherry-wood crinoline armchair attributed to Eliphalet Chapin, a Connecticut cabinetmaker who worked between 1780-1795.* RIGHT: *Master cabinetmakers usually used mahogany for furniture made in the Chippendale manner. Therefore, collectors call pieces fashioned of walnut, as is this shell-carved bonnet-top highboy from Connecticut, "country Chippendale."*

Windsor brace-back side chairs made in an 18th century Rhode Island shop.

ing them from fruitwood and advertising them as "the best and cheapest that can be bought." As early as 1770, Randolph was urging prospective customers to buy American-made goods because importing merchandise from England was "inconsistent with the true interests" of the colonies.

Randolph served as a member of the Philadelphia City Troop, furnishing his own uniform, horse and equipment, and crossed the Delaware River with Washington on Christmas Eve, 1775. When Thomas Jefferson first came to Philadelphia as a delegate to the Continental Congress, he stayed with Randolph. During his visit Jefferson showed his host a plan for a small portable desk. Randolph made the desk and Jefferson wrote the Declaration of Independence on it.

While such Philadelphia craftsmen as Jonathan Gostelowe, John Folwell, Thomas Tufft, James Gillingham, and William Savery—to name but a few—specialized in beautifully constructed and elaborately carved furniture, others were catering to those who could not afford high prices. These men sought trade by advertising as shown by this notice in the Pennsylvania *Gazette* for September 5, 1765:

Made and sold by Josiah Sherald at the sign of the Gold-headed Cane, in Second-street, a little below Dock Bridge, All Sorts of Rush-bottom chairs, Windsor Chairs, Couches, Canes &c. made in the best Manner, and Newest Fashions, which he will sell low for Cash or short Credit . . . the said Sherald will barter chairs for Goods at Cash Prices.

The Windsor chair mentioned above originated in England. It was first made by wheelwrights who shaped its legs and spindles with draw-shaves as they did spokes, bent its arms in the same manner as they formed wheel rims, and substituted a plank seat for a hub. Traditionally, Windsors became fashionable when George III of England was caught in a sudden rainstorm and took refuge in a cottage near the town of Windsor and found the stout wooden chair in which he sat so comfortable that he asked permission to take it to the royal castle. It is a good story but not true. Chairmakers were selling Windsors forty years before George ascended his throne.

Nine distinct varieties of Windsors were made in America—all better constructed and more stylish than their English counterparts. The Windsor became very popular. It was John Adam's favorite chair, while Washington bought twenty-four "ovel Back Chairs" for the porch at Mount Vernon. They were constructed by Gilbert Gaw of Philadelphia (where the finest Windsors were produced) for forty-four dollars.

Francis Trumble, who shipped furniture from Philadelphia to the West Indies, also received an important order for Windsors. It was to replace the furniture he had first made for Independence Hall. During the occupation of the building as a prison and hospital from September, 1777, to June, 1778, British soldiers had kept warm by burning Trumble's original furniture.

Famous as Philadelphia was for its simple Windsor chairs, that city's "Gentlemen Cabinet and Chair Makers" did not lose their reputation for producing richly ornamented mahogany furniture. However, craftsmen elsewhere were also creating furniture that was both well-designed and beautifully carved. In Salem, Massachusetts, Samuel McIntire was not only

LEFT: *Windsor curly maple comb-back armchair. Horseshoe crest rail on turned spindles, with eight-spindle crest; flaring saddle seat; turned legs with cross stretcher ending in lion feet. Pennsylvania 18th century. The 18th-century maple and curly maple tavern table is noteworthy because of its splayed, turned, and stretched legs.* RIGHT: *Although the finest Windsor chairs were produced in Philadelphia, this Windsor writing armchair made in New England late in the 18th century is the work of a master chairmaker.*

LEFT: *Thomas Sheraton, last of the great English furniture designers, had a strong influence on New England cabinetmakers. Constructed in Boston about 1810, this Sheraton inlaid satinwood and mahogany secretary-cabinet has tambour shutters concealing a drawer and pigeonholes.* RIGHT: *Sheraton inlaid mahogany and satinwood secretary-cabinet with tambour front attributed to John Seymour.*

making furniture but also ornamenting mantels, doors, and stair railings, while in New York City, Gilbert Ash was fashioning some of the finest Chippendale-style chairs ever made in this country, and there were others who displayed outstanding skill.

With the outbreak of the Revolution, cabinetmakers in every colony laid down their tools and picked up muskets. John Folwell, Jonathan Gostelow, and Hercules Courtenay of Philadelphia held commissions in the Continental Army, while Quaker David Evans, whose religion forbade him to bear arms, made tent poles, camp chairs, and cot bedsteads for use in the field. John Dunlap, a member of a family of well-known New Hampshire cabinetmakers, became a major, and Stephen Badlam served as a captain of artillery, later rising to be general of the Massachusetts Militia. In 1776, Marius Willet, the famous New York City chairmaker, led the Sons of Liberty when they raided the wagon train carrying supplies to the British troops in Boston, and two years later he played an important part in defeating Burgoyne.

Benjamin Frothingham was typical of these soldier-craftsmen. Boston born, Frothingham operated his shop in nearby Charlestown and, as a young man, joined the expedition to capture Quebec in 1775. He then became a major in the colonial army. While all American cabinetmakers suffered during the Revolution, Frothingham and his fellow craftsmen in Charlestown experienced the greatest loss. Angered because the colonists had fortified Bunker Hill, General Gage, the British commander in Boston, set fire to Charlestown on June 17, 1775, destroying most of the settlement including the shops of Frothingham and twenty-eight other furniture makers. Their claim for damages was never paid.

Fortunately, Frothingham—unlike many of his associates—was able to resume operations immediately after the Revolution, having inherited a considerable estate from his father, Benjamin, Sr., who was also a cabinetmaker. Major Ben—as the younger Frothingham was known after his military service—made block-front furniture nearly equal in quality to that produced in Newport, although its ornamentation was much less ornate. As active socially as he was in business, Frothingham was a close friend of Paul Revere and of George Washington. When the latter visited Boston in 1789, the only private call he made was to Frothingham's home.

However, the best-known designer and maker of furniture of the post-Revolutionary period is John Seymour of Boston, who, with his son, Thomas, produced pieces made of several different kinds of woods, including many with tambour doors—flexible sliding panels made by glueing thin strips of wood to a linen background. Seymour is also famous for painting the insides of drawers and compartments a robin's egg blue.

When the Revolution ended, great numbers of Europeans migrated to America. Among them were the Fifes. Hardworking folk, they had scrimped and saved to pay their passage from Scotland to the New World. They settled in Albany, New York, in 1784, and it was in that city that their sixteen-year-old son Duncan was apprenticed to a cabinetmaker.

No one knows if the young Scot impressed his master, for there is no record of Duncan's apprenticeship. However, the lad must have shown great ability while learning the skills of his chosen craft because he became the maker of the finest furniture produced in this country during the first quarter of the nineteenth century. Moreover, he is the only American cabinetmaker whose name is associated with all types of furniture.

After serving his apprenticeship, Fife conducted his own shop in Albany but soon decided that there were more opportunities in New York City. Therefore, he moved there and established himself at 2 Broad Street in the heart of the furniture-making district. The New York City Directory for 1792 lists him as a joiner, while the Directory of 1794 classifies him as a cabinetmaker and gives his address as 3 Broad Street. The 1794 listing also shows that Duncan had changed the spelling of his last name from Fife to Phyfe. But his fortunes had not changed. Although he had secured a few orders, he was no better off than if he had stayed in Albany. Phyfe needed far more work than he was getting, for now he had a wife to support, Rachel Lowzade, whom he married in 1793.

Phyfe's financial worries vanished when he was commissioned to make furniture for the daughter of John Jacob Astor, the wealthy fur merchant whose trading post had helped establish the claim of the United States to Oregon in a boundary dispute with England. When the furniture was delivered, the Astors were so pleased with it that they recommended Phyfe's shop to all their friends. As the Astors were among the leaders of New York society, Phyfe soon found himself busy "making fashionable furniture for fashionable people."

To assist him in filling the ever-increasing demand for his furniture,

ABOVE: *Both these carved, gilded mirrors were made about 1800. One is a two-eagle girandole, the other has a river landscape painted on the panel.* RIGHT: *Slipper-footed tea table made from maple, a wood commonly used by early 18th century New England cabinetmakers for the so-called Queen Anne furniture.*

BELOW LEFT: *18th century drop-leaf table in the Queen Anne manner fashioned from walnut, the traditional wood for furniture in this style.* RIGHT: *Demicartouche-shaped tapestry marble-top table dating from the Federal Period (1790-1830).*

Phyfe engaged some experienced craftsmen and accepted several apprentices. However, he soon discovered that his shop was too small for so many workmen, so he moved to a well-lighted and spacious store at 35 Partition Street. While Duncan—"a very plain man, always working and always smoking a short pipe"—attended to business downstairs, Rachel went about her household duties on the second floor.

Now that he could afford them, Phyfe purchased copies of English design books and adapted the patterns in them to meet his needs. Meanwhile, Americans who had not forgotten the aid given the colonies by France during their struggle to win freedom from England were showing great enthusiasm for French fashions. As a result, the style now known as Directoire, based on the designs of the famous French artist, David, became very popular. The term Directoire itself is derived from Directory, the name given to the group of men who conducted the government after the French Revolution.

Phyfe appropriated the best features of the Directoire style, just as he borrowed the finest elements in the patterns of the famous English cabinetmakers. From them he created an originality of design and worked in so individual a manner that he evolved a style of his own. At first, he used plain turned legs on his handiwork, but today, furniture experts can identify his creations by the appearance of the leg. Phyfe usually ended a leg with a brass lion's foot (he imported a great deal of his brassware from England) or a carved wooden dog's leg.

The front legs of Phyfe's chairs curve forward and the rear ones swing backward from the top rail to the floor, for Phyfe always preferred to use a curved line rather than a straight one. His chair arms are curved as are their supports which are scrolled, carved, or delicately turned in an urnlike

Drawing made about 1820 of Duncan Phyfe's shop and warehouse.

shape. At times Phyfe made the front legs of a chair round and curved, and the back ones square. But he often reversed this pattern, never placing any carving on the rear legs.

A master of decorative detail, Phyfe ornamented practically every piece of his furniture with semicircular molded projections technically known as reeding. He also placed carvings of wheat, acanthus leaves, plumes, cornucopias, oak branches, and thunderbolts on his creations. His favorite design for a chair back was a lyre and he also used representations of this ancient musical instrument as a support for tables, making the strings from brass or whalebone, and the pin, which runs through the top, of ebony.

Phyfe made many different kinds of tables. They ranged from pedestal and four-legged tables to card tables with five legs—the extra leg swings out to support the extended leaf when in use. He also fashioned beds, dressing glasses, footstools, sideboards, sofas, piano stands, and window benches, all beautifully proportioned.

Mahogany was Phyfe's favorite wood. He preferred the reddish-tinged variety native to the West Indies and spent hours examining hundreds of logs before choosing one. However, he would quickly offer as much as a thousand dollars for a single log if it met his standards. Such a timber, when sawed into boards and made into furniture, brought him many times that amount, for Phyfe commanded high prices for his work, receiving as much as $122 for a sofa—which was considered extremely expensive at the time.

By now Phyfe's reputation had spread far beyond New York City, and he was shipping furniture all over the country. Agents represented him in various Southern cities; his relative, Lachlan Phyfe, acting as his inter-

The lyre, an ancient decorating motif, was frequently used by Phyfe for chair backs and table bases.

LEFT: *Carved mahogany and rose crimson ciselé velvet soft made by Duncan Phyfe. Typical of the master's work, it has a crest rail carved with bowknotted and tasseled drapery swags flanked by bowknotted sheaves. The reeded scroll arms have foliated and reeded frontal supports, continuing to matching round tapering legs.* RIGHT: *Carved mahogany arm chair made by Duncan Phyfe. It has an incurvate fluted crest rail above X-shaped splat between reeded and scroll uprights, on reeded, round legs.*

mediary in Baltimore. To meet the needs of his expanding business, Phyfe purchased two more buildings on Partition Street. In 1816, Partition Street was renamed Fulton Street in honor of Robert Fulton, the American inventor of the first successful steamboat. Today, Phyfe's property is the site of the Hudson Terminal Building.

When Empire—a style of furniture inspired by Napoleon, who commanded French artists and craftsmen to carry it out—became popular on this side of the Atlantic, Phyfe, who combined the skills of a craftsman with the common sense of a businessman, took up the new fad. However, his work was far more delicate than its European counterpart. He now employed over one hundred journeymen, master cabinetmakers, turners, and carvers and probably was not making a great deal of furniture himself. Yet he continued to supervise the cutting of veneer from carefully selected mahogany logs. By matching or contrasting the grain of these thin layers which were glued crosswise upon less attractively grained wood, Phyfe's workmen, under his direction, created exquisite ornamentation on all types of American Empire furniture.

A quiet and methodical individual, Phyfe took little part in social life, nor did he seek publicity. The only time he seems to have been prominent in public affairs was when he was commissioned to construct a cabinet to hold bottles of water from Lake Erie which were presented to Lafayette as a souvenir when the Erie Canal was opened in 1825. At the same time he also made cedar boxes to contain the medals cast to commemorate this historic event.

In 1837, two of Phyfe's sons, Michael and James, joined the business which was now known as Duncan Phyfe and Sons. When Michael died in 1840, the firm was renamed Duncan Phyfe and Son. Meanwhile, furniture styles had again changed, but Phyfe rebelled against the new fashion which called for massive furniture either covered with veneer or elaborately ornamented. Eventually, however, in order to continue operations, he was forced to produce what he derisively referred to as "butcher furniture."

But he did not work in this style very long. In 1847, Phyfe retired and sold his stock at auction. To keep busy he made small pieces of furniture for his family and friends and managed the properties he had acquired over the years in New York City and Brooklyn, which were then worth about $100,000. He continued to live on Fulton Street and it was there, in 1854, that Duncan Phyfe, the most celebrated and most imitated American cabinetmaker, died at the age of eighty-six.

While Phyfe is the best known cabinetmaker of his time, other men were producing excellent furniture during the same period. Certain craftsmen paid Phyfe the compliment of attempting to copy his style, while still others, among them John Budd of New York City, did not imitate the master although their work shows his influence. Meanwhile, such woodworkers as Hugo and John Finlay of Baltimore developed styles of their own. The Finlays also carried out the designs of Benjamin Henry Latrobe, the architect commissioned by James Madison to remodel the "president's

State landmark sign outside the Hitchcock chair factory in Riverton (Hitchcocks-ville), Connecticut.

A photograph of the original Hitchcock factory before restoration work commenced in 1946. The last chairs were made here about the time of the Civil War.

house" after it was burnt by the British during the War of 1812. Latrobe, incidentally, is responsible for the popular name for the official residence of the president of the United States—The White House. He covered some of the damage done by the fire with several coats of white paint.

The Finlays specialized in painted furniture. This was not a new style, for "fancy chairs"—chairs of light construction sometimes solidly painted and, at others, decorated with striping or scenes in color or gold leaf—had been advertised in New York City as early as 1795. Because these chairs were originally designed for drawing and music rooms in the homes of the wealthy, they were built by skilled workmen and ornamented by trained artists. This made them quite expensive. However, by 1825, fancy chairs were in common use, thanks to mass production methods which enabled them to be sold cheaply.

No one was more responsible for flooding the market with low-priced fancy chairs than Lambert Hitchcock, who was born in Cheshire, Connecti-

31

cut, June 28, 1795. In 1818, when he was twenty-three years old, Hitchcock moved to the little village of Barkhamsted in western Connecticut and opened a small factory in which he manufactured chair parts.

The first to cater to the "do-it-yourself" trade, Hitchcock shipped thousands of his knocked-down chairs to seaboard cities in the South. He also sold chair kits to traveling peddlers—suppliers of all kinds of merchandise to countryfolk—who assembled them for their customers.

Hitchcock's business flourished and soon he was sending chair parts to dealers in Detroit and Chicago as well as his southern outlets. To meet the demand for his unassembled chairs, Hitchcock had to hire more help and his factory became the center of a bustling community known as Hitchcocksville.

In 1825, Hitchcock stopped making chair parts and began manufacturing complete fancy chairs, and ever since has been wrongly credited with originating the type of chair that bears his name. Actually, inexpensive painted chairs decorated with stenciled designs in gold and colors were turned out by numerous makers. But because Hitchcock clearly labeled his product "L. Hitchcock, Hitchcocksville, Connecticut, Warrented," and other man-

An early example of mass production—Lambert Hitchcock's inexpensive decorated chair.

Old photograph taken at the Hitchcock factory. Note the handicapped workmen.

ufacturers rarely stamped their chairs with their names, Hitchcock has been popularly accepted as the creator of a type of chair.

All so-called Hitchcock chairs, no matter who made them, have certain characteristics. Usually the frame is birch or oak, and the rush, cane, or wooden seat is broader in front than at the back, while its front edge is rounded to make it more comfortable. The front legs and the front rung are turned in spool, ring, or vase shapes, but the back legs, which extend above the seat to form the uprights of the back, are plain. Several different designs were used in forming the back slat but all are wide and curved and generally there is a narrow crosspiece below them. While the main ornamentation is on the back slat—horns of plenty, bunches of grapes, flowers, birds, and other decorative motifs—the turnings of the legs and other parts of these chairs are touched with gilt.

A conscientious chairmaker, Hitchcock was sincere when he placed "Warrented" on his product. He carefully selected all the wood used in his factory, traveling great distances to inspect the offerings of lumbermen, and gave orders to his employees to discard any wood containing imperfections. Moreover, he insisted upon careful workmanship. As a result, customers got full value when they paid a dollar and a half for one of Hitchcock's chairs.

They were bought by the thousands and, to increase production, Hitchcock built a three-story brick factory in which he employed over one hundred men, women, and children. Often entire families worked for him.

33

While the men operated wood-working machinery and assembled chairs, their wives and children did the painting and decorating.

After the children had applied an undercoat of Venetian red or lemon-yellow to the chairs, a crew of women, using a technique that permitted faint streaks of the undercoat to show, painted them a glossy black. Other women, using paper stencils, then decorated the chairs. Rubbing their finger tips in oil, they used them to pick up dry gold, silver, or bronze powder and, by smearing the powder over the stencil, transferred the design to the chair. Then, with a brush, they painted the birds, flowers, or fruit in the design in their natural colors.

By 1828, Hitchcock was manufacturing fifteen thousand chairs a year but was having trouble collecting from his customers. Then, too, the competition of other makers was cutting into his profits. Finally, he was forced into bankruptcy in July, 1829, and the factory was turned over to four trustees by the court. The trustees immediately hired Hitchcock as their agent and within three years he had managed matters so well that he paid off his debts and the factory was returned to him.

Hitchcock acquired a partner as well as going bankrupt in 1829. He was Arba Alford, Jr., who had worked in the factory from the first, rising to the post of general manager. The partners became brothers-in-law in 1830 when Alford's sister, Eunice, married Hitchcock. The two men had an ideal working arrangement. While Hitchcock went about the country selling chairs, Alford supervised the factory. In 1834, when Hitchcock was elected to the state legislature—but politics never interfered with selling trips—he and his wife moved to Hartford.

The partnership was dissolved in 1843, and Hitchcock then opened a factory in Unionville, Connecticut, where he made chairs identical to those being made at Hitchcocksville under the direction of Arba Alford and his brother, Alfred. However, Hitchcock's new venture failed.

Modern manufacturing methods are ignored at the rebuilt Hitchcock chair factory and chairs are still made in the traditional manner.

Slipper chair attributed to John Belter.

Typical Belter craftsmanship: a pair of rosewood and ecru side chairs. The frames are carved with C-scrolls; floral clusters ornament the cabriole legs; the backs and seats are cartouche-shaped.

Belter sofa upholstered in rich rose brocade with carvings in rosewood of leaves, flowers, and fruit.

Hitchcock died in Unionville in 1852. Meanwhile, the Alfords had closed down the factory and later sold the building. After being used for various purposes, it lay vacant for some time and then was reopened as a chair factory. Today, the "fancy chairs" made there reproduce in every detail the original ones, including the famous stenciled label "L. Hitchcock, Hitchcocksville, Connecticut, Warrented."

Although Hitchcock's name is associated with a straight chair, he also manufactured rocking chairs of various types. Historians are agreed that the rocking chair is an American invention—none were made in Europe until 1840—but its originator is unknown. Tradition holds that Benjamin Franklin was the first to put rockers on a chair, because he was known to have owned in 1787 ". . . a great armed chair with rockers, and a large fan placed over it, with which he fans himself and keeps off flies. . . ."

However, there is a record of an earlier rocking chair than Franklin's. It is a bill dated February 11, 1774, "to bottoming a rocking chair" sent to a customer by William Savery, the famous Quaker cabinetmaker of Philadelphia. This must have been an old chair for it needed repair, but it could have been a straight chair to which rockers had been added. Most rocking chairs before 1800 were of this type, as shown by the charge of one shilling sixpence Daniel Ross of Ipswich, Massachusetts, made in September, 1787, for "putting rockers to a chair."

By the end of the first quarter of the nineteenth century, semi-skilled workmen in large factories equipped with machinery were producing furniture that could be sold cheaply, and the art of cabinetmaking declined. However, while men argued over slavery, fought a war to end it, and then turned their attention to the problem of peace, a few craftsmen continued to carry on the traditions of those who worked with their hands.

Perhaps the best known of this group is John Henry Belter, who was born in Germany in 1804. After learning cabinetmaking and wood-carving as an apprentice in Wittenberg, famous as the home of Martin Luther, leader of the Reformation, Belter came to the United States. He opened a shop in Chatham Square in 1844, then the center of New York City's cabinetmaking district. He must have done well, for he married Louisa Springmeyer the same year.

Eventually, Belter operated a five-story furniture factory on Third Avenue with his four brothers-in-law who had become his partners in 1856. J. H. Belter and Company was a large organization, Belter staffing it with a crew of expert carvers he imported from the Black Forest region of Germany, and indenturing forty apprentices.

Belter himself was an excellent craftsman excelling in carving intricate patterns in high relief. All his furniture was elaborate, but his sofas and

Modern designers draw upon the traditional lines of these fine pieces: ABOVE: Carving on this walnut corner chair from Rhode Island shows it was made toward the end of the Queen Anne period. TOP RIGHT: A mahogany slant-top desk made in New York City is richly carved as is much Chippendale-style furniture. RIGHT: Mahogany bow-front, Hepplewhite-style chest of drawers. BELOW: A Connecticut-made, early 19th century inlaid cherrywood sideboard in the Hepplewhite style.

Early 19th century carved mahogany three-pedestal dining table whose maker was influenced by the designs in Sheraton's Drawing Book.

chairs were the most ornate, usually being upholstered in richly-hued brocades and damasks. Frequently, Belter gilded his carvings of leaves, fruit, flowers, or lace-like scrolls which gave them the appearance of sculptured metal. He never repeated a design even when fashioning a matching set of furniture—each piece would vary slightly in ornamentation. Belter's technique has never been equaled, and although most of his creations are lush, they are, at the same time, both practical and comfortable.

Most of Belter's furniture was made of rosewood—a general name for a group of tropical trees. While rosewood with its dark-red or purplish color-streaked with black was Belter's favorite, it was difficult to carve or to bend into the curves that are characteristic of his chairs and sofas. By experimentation, Belter devised a process of laminating rosewood which made it easy to bend and, at the same time, added to its strength. His method—for which he received a patent in 1856—was to glue several thin layers of rosewood together, the layers being placed so that their grains were at right angles. Today, plywood is laminated in the same manner.

There never was a sufficient supply of rosewood for Belter's needs. Therefore, he only used it to make choice pieces and fashioned much of his other work from black walnut, for wood milled from this native and common tree could be made to resemble imported rosewood if treated with certain chemicals. However, Belter took as much care when making furniture from black walnut, or with various hard woods stained to simulate ebony, as he did when using expensive tropical cabinet woods. But it is his richly figured rosewood furniture that has brought him fame.

On September 15, 1863, Belter, who for some unknown reason had been systematically destroying most of his patterns, visited his lawyer and drew up his will. Four days later he died. His brothers-in-law continued the business until December, 1867, when they were forced into bankruptcy. After the firm's books were audited, Belter's equity amounted to $20,000, but bad debts and mortgages reduced this amount to $2,500. Nevertheless, while John Henry Belter, unlike Phyfe, did not leave his heirs a fortune, he was one of America's greatest cabinetmakers and wood carvers.

Following the War Between the States, furniture factories were established wherever there was water power and an ample supply of wood. Typical of these cities was Grand Rapids, Michigan, where, in 1836, William Haldans founded the furniture industry which was to make that city world famous. By 1877, mass-produced furniture from Grand Rapids and other manufacturing centers dominated the market and *The American Cabinet Maker*, a trade journal, reported: "The days are gone, never to return, when an individual art workman could be employed on an individual piece of furniture to do what he liked with it."

But some people did not like machine-produced furniture. Magazine writers, prompted by William Morris, the English artist, and Charles L. Eastlake, the British critic, railed against the poor taste of furniture makers, while Harriet Beecher Stowe, the author of *Uncle Tom's Cabin*, even suggested that women refuse to accept the then current furniture styles. Actually, there was no definite style during this period—furniture makers thought nothing of combining traditional patterns with "modern" ornamentation, suggesting the use of bamboo easy chairs along with massive cabinets covered with marquetry, or reproducing colonial furniture in bleached oak. In fact, from 1870 to 1890, American furniture style was a conglomeration of everything from early Greek to late Victorian.

Then, as the nineteenth century ended, a group of young designers became exponents of *L'Art Nouveau*—which got its inspiration from nature. When furniture ornamented with simple carvings of natural objects was exhibited by this group at the Paris *Exposition Universelles* in 1901, it attracted wide attention. Within a few years a number of Americans, including David Walcott Randall, Thomas Hadley, George Pike, and Paul

Resting on claw and ball feet this carved mahogany drop-leaf table shows Chippendale's influence on Rhode Island cabinetmakers.

Maryland cabinetmakers were masters of the art of inlay as shown by this Hepplewhite mahogany hunt board made in Baltimore about 1820.

A Chippendale carved mahogany shell- and tassel-back side chair with the cabriole leg characteristic of American-made furniture in this style.

Pre-Revolutionary carved mahogany tilt-top tripod table with "bird-cage" support, made by Philadelphia craftsmen.

Frankl, were creating furniture which blended the chaste beauty of classic styles with the functional demands of modern living.

Today, their successors, employing traditional cabinet woods, plastics, modern metals, and time-tested fabrics, create furniture which, although factory produced, is proof that Frank Lloyd Wright, the famous architect, was correct in maintaining that: "the machine is a tool of man, man is not a tool of the machine."

3
Clockmakers

What is a clock? Technically, it is a machine that records the passing of time and also strikes at least the hours, while any other device that simply shows the time—such as the portable time-telling machine we call a watch—is known as a "timepiece." Both clocks and timepieces consist of a train of wheels driven by the uncoiling of a spring, a falling weight, or other means —the speed of the turning wheels being kept at a uniform rate in various ways—while the wheels move hands around a dial which has been scaled to indicate units of time.

Long before man learned to make clocks and watches, the residents of the ancient centers of civilization—where the sun normally shines every day —used sundials to measure time. Although traders introduced sundials into other lands at a very early date, they were of little value in regions subject to unsettled weather. As a result, wise men sought a means of recording time mechanically. Their search resulted in the invention of the clepsydra, or water clock.

There were many different kinds of water clocks, but all operated on the same principle—the flow of water from one vessel to another marked the passage of time. The clepsydra used in Roman courts to limit the length of speeches was very simple. It consisted of a jar of known capacity, pierced at the bottom with small holes through which the water escaped. When the jar was empty, the speaker had to stop talking. On the other hand, the water clock Charlemagne sent to the King of Persia as a gift in A.D. 807 was a far more complicated device, for, in addition to marking time, it also struck the hours.

Among other early methods for measuring time were especially made candles and a quantity of sand encased in two pear-shaped glass bulbs connected to one another by a narrow neck and supported by a frame. The candles were exactly twelve inches long and burnt down one inch every twenty minutes. While it normally took an hour for the sand to empty from the top bulb to the bottom one—hence, the name, hourglass—it took two hours for the sand in some of these timepieces to pass from the upper to the lower glass. Still others, used for specific purposes, marked the passage of seconds or of minutes.

No one knows for sure where or when the wheel clock was invented. Some authorities give the credit to the famous Roman scholar Boethius and the year as A.D. 510. Others claim the honor for Pope Sylvester II in A.D. 996. However, it is universally agreed that wheel clocks were well known in Europe by the thirteenth century.

Nevertheless, hourglasses and sundials—both fixed and pocket size—were in common use in colonial America. Perhaps the most famous owner of a portable sundial was Roger Williams, the founder of Rhode Island, who came to this country in 1631. Over one hundred years later an advertisement in the *Boston Gazette and Country Journal* offered "one fourth, one half minute, one half hour and two hour glasses." But long before the publication of this advertisement, wheel clocks were ticking in homes throughout British North America. Many of them had been made by native craftsmen, while others had been imported from London, then the clockmaking center of the world.

LEFT: *Before the invention of the wheel clock, men had tried many methods of telling time, including sundials, water clocks, and hourglasses.* RIGHT: *Tower clock of the Old Sturbridge Village Meetinghouse, Sturbridge, Massachusetts, made by Edward Howard, an apprentice of Aaron Willard, Jr.*

Because clocks were expensive in the 1600's, many people relied on tower clocks to tell them the time. These clocks get their name from the custom of placing them in a tower, church steeple, or on the sides of public buildings. On July 28, 1684, the authorities of Boston "Agreed with Wm Sumner blacksmith to pay him 4lds in mony to keepe the clocke at ye North end of the Towne for one yeare to begin the 1st of Augt next & to pay him for worke done about sd clocke the yeare past, 14s, mony."

It seems strange that a blacksmith was commissioned "to keepe the clocke" in 1684, because William Davis, an English clockmaker, had established a shop in Boston the previous year. Davis, arriving in Boston "understocked with money, but overstocked with family," was forced to find a taxpayer who would guarantee that he would not become a public charge, and David Edwards accepted the responsibility. James Batterson was just as fortunate. After operating shops in Philadelphia, New York City, and Charlestown, South Carolina, Batterson migrated to Boston in 1707 with empty pockets. An entry in the Boston Town Records for September 29, 1707, reveals his lack of funds: "James Batterson, Clockmaker being present Says he came from Pensilvania into theis Town abt a month Since & desires to dwell here. the Select men do now warn him to depart out of Town to fine Suretyes to Save the Town from Charge."

Where Batterson found his "Suretyes" is unknown, but within a month he was advertising that "James Batterson lately arrived from London" had opened a clockmaking shop. It must have been a successful venture for Batterson worked at his craft until his death in 1727. Meanwhile, other clockmakers had established themselves in Boston. Among these was Benjamin Bagnall, an English-born Quaker who became a prominent merchant and real estate dealer.

Bagnall had served his apprenticeship in Philadelphia, home of many famous clockmakers. Abel Cottey, a fellow-passenger of William Penn aboard the *Welcome* in 1682, was probably the first of his craft to set up shop in the colonies. Like most early American clockmakers, Cottey made tall clocks—commonly called "grandfather" clocks. However, they usually only fabricated the works and dial, the case which enclosed the movement, pendulum, and weights (and kept out the dust) being fashioned by a cabinetmaker. The taste of the individual cabinetmaker determined the design of a case and the wood used in its construction. This was also true of the so-called dwarf tall clocks, nicknamed "grandmother" clocks, which were four feet or less in height but which retained the exact proportions of tall clocks, some of which were nine feet high.

As indicated, pre-Revolutionary Philadelphia supported a large number of outstanding clockmakers, including, among others, Christopher Sower,

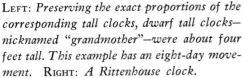

LEFT: *Preserving the exact proportions of the corresponding tall clocks, dwarf tall clocks— nicknamed "grandmother"—were about four feet tall. This example has an eight-day movement.* RIGHT: *A Rittenhouse clock.*

four generations of the Gorgas family, the Chandlee family, Robert Leslie, and Edward Duffield. The latter, a close friend of Benjamin Franklin and an executor of his will, was constantly interrupted while working by passers-by who entered his shop and asked the time, as few people owned watches. Annoyed at being disturbed, Duffield made a clock with a double face—so that it could be read from both directions—and hung it out of a second-story window.

But of all Philadelphia clockmakers, David Rittenhouse was the most skillful. He probably inherited his mechanical ability from his great-grandfather, William Ritterhuysen, an immigrant from Holland who established, in 1690, the first paper mill in America at Germantown, Pennsylvania, where David was born on April 8, 1732. As a boy, young Rittenhouse worked long hours on his father's farm, but he managed to find time to teach himself higher mathematics and to study astronomy. There is also a possibility that his uncle, John Gorgas, accepted him as an apprentice and taught him the craft of clockmaking. But whether Rittenhouse received any formal training or not, he began making tall clocks and scientific instruments in Norristown, Pennsylvania, when he was only nineteen years old.

45

A most competent mechanic, Rittenhouse not only fashioned extremely accurate clocks for his customers but also employed his talents to make far more complicated ones for his own amusement. Perhaps his most intricate clock is the one having six dials which he assembled in 1767, now displayed by a Philadelphia museum. The main dial shows the phases of the moon and has four hands which indicate seconds, minutes, hours, and days (including the twenty-ninth of February in leap years). Other dials show the orbits of the planets around the sun; the revolution of the moon about the earth; the movements of Saturn; and whether sun time is faster or slower than meridian time. The sixth dial describes the chime combinations which sound every quarter-hour—any one of ten tunes can be chosen by pressing a knob.

Among the scientific instruments constructed by Rittenhouse were at least two orrerys—planetariums which illustrate the relative positions and motions of solar bodies by the rotation and revolution of balls moved by wheels. He fabricated one in 1757, when he was only twenty-three years old, and sold it to Princeton University. In 1770, he built another which was much larger and more scientifically accurate for the University of Pennsylvania.

Besides fashioning clocks, orrerys, and other scientific apparatus, Rittenhouse worked as a surveyor. He assisted Charles Mason and Jeremiah Dixon in establishing the boundary line which ended the dispute between

Rittenhouse orrery made for the University of Pennsylvania and now displayed in the university's Charles Patterson Van Pelt Library.

the Penn family, proprietors of Pennsylvania, and the Calverts, owners of Maryland. Today, the Mason-Dixon Line not only serves as the physical southern boundary of Pennsylvania and the northern boundary of Maryland, Delaware, and West Virginia, but also as the symbolic division between the North and South.

In 1769, the American Philosophical Society commissioned Rittenhouse to observe the transit of Venus—the passage of the planet across the sun—and he erected a temporary observatory for the purpose in the Pennsylvania state house. The following year he moved to Philadelphia where he continued to manufacture clocks and scientific machines. During the Revolution Rittenhouse served the colonial cause in various ways and, with the coming of peace, became Treasurer of Pennsylvania. In 1779, he was appointed professor of astronomy at the University of Pennsylvania, which had been founded by Benjamin Franklin, whom he succeeded as President of the American Philosophical Society in 1791. The following year, Rittenhouse accepted the post of Director of the United States Mint, holding that office until 1795. Meanwhile, he received honors from learned societies on both sides of the Atlantic and was active in time-recording experiments until his death on June 26, 1796.

Whether they worked in large communities or in crossroad settlements, pre-Revolutionary clockmakers employed the same techniques. Using hammer, drill, and file, they hand-fashioned gears from brass plates they had cast in sand molds. After casting the brass blanks and allowing them to cool, the craftsmen hammered them for days to stiffen the soft metal, then filed and polished the brass to the required thickness. Finally, the teeth of the gears were cut with a file.

Because of the scarcity of brass in the colonies, clockmakers constantly advertised for old metal which they could recast. In time, they were able to purchase brass blanks from Europe or obtain them from local foundries. But fashioning gears continued to be a tedious process because they had to be cut and filed by hand. As a result, it took months to make a clock and no clockmaker began the task unless he had a definite order from a customer. Therefore, it was necessary for many clockmakers to engage in other activities in order to support themselves. Ezra Dodge of New London, Connecticut, informed the public that although he ". . . still carries on Clock and Watchmaking," his shop was stocked with a "General assortment of groceries, rum, brandy and flour."

In 1781, Isaac Doolittle of New Haven, Connecticut, advertised "Compasses, Sea and Land Surveyors scales and protractors, gauging rods, walking sticks, Silver and Plated Buttons turned upon a horn, also Clocks and Watches, etc." A considerable number of early clockmakers were also sil-

47

ABOVE: *Because the accurately firing, fast-loading rifle made by gunsmiths in Lancaster County, Pennsylvania, became the favorite weapon of Daniel Boone and other early explorers, it became known as the "Kentucky rifle."* RIGHT: *Benjamin Willard made this tall clock which is enclosed in a cherrywood case of Sheraton design.* BELOW: *An early surveyor's instrument of New England origin. Many clockmakers had to increase their earnings by making other items besides clocks.*

versmiths or operated a blacksmith forge. Among the latter was David Blaisdell, one of a family of twelve clockmakers. Blaisdell worked in Amesbury, Massachusetts, and was commissioned to fashion much of the metal work for the vessels built in that town for the colonial army.

An advertisement in an Annapolis, Maryland, newspaper in 1764 announced that Charles Willson Peale "Makes, cleans and repairs clocks and mends watches as well as carrying on the saddler's Business." But Peale, a clever silversmith and wood carver who is credited with being the first person in this country to make sets of artificial teeth, soon abandoned clockmaking and his other activities to study painting under John Singleton Copley, America's first outstanding artist, and also to become a student at the Royal Academy in London. In 1772, Peale painted the first portrait of Washington ever executed, depicting him in the uniform of a colonel of the Virginia militia. Peale also painted pictures of other prominent men and established an academy of fine arts in Philadelphia.

Gunsmithing was a favorite sideline of many clockmakers and, at the outbreak of the Revolution, they melted down the lead weights they had cast for clocks and molded the metal into bullets and used their mechanical skill to make arms. A large number closed their shops and served the cause of freedom as soldiers.

With the coming of peace, clockmakers returned to their craft. However, there was little demand for their handiwork. Not only was money scarce but also clocks were too expensive for the average householder. An eight-day movement for a tall clock made by a country craftsman sold for about forty dollars, a very large sum in those days, while those made by better-known clockmakers were considerably higher. Moreover, the case alone could be quite costly if it were made of imported wood and constructed by a master cabinetmaker.

Anxious to secure more trade, American clockmakers began to make smaller clocks which could be sold more cheaply than tall clocks. Among those who helped bring about the transition from standing clocks to wall and shelf clocks was the Willard family of Massachusetts. While over a dozen Willards made their name famous in clockmaking history, the most outstanding are the three sons of Benjamin Willard, Sr., a descendant of Colonel Simon Willard who founded Concord, Massachusetts.

Oldest of the Willard brothers was Benjamin, Jr., who was born in Grafton, Massachusetts, in 1743. After serving his apprenticeship under Benjamin Cheney, the senior member of a well-known Connecticut clockmaking family, young Willard opened a shop in Grafton. Later he moved to Lexington and then to Roxbury, now a part of Boston, but also maintained his Grafton shop. Readers of the *Massachusetts Spy* and other newspapers became familiar with Willard's advertisement in which he described "A number of Musical Clocks which play a different Tune each Day in the Week, on Sunday a Psalm Tune." However, although Benjamin Willard warranted his clocks to "measure Time without Variation, and to go many Years without cleaning," he was not as accomplished a craftsman as his brother, Simon.

Simon was born in Grafton on April 3, 1753. He received very little education but showed great mechanical ability as a boy. Benjamin, Jr., taught him the rudiments of clockmaking and a "Mr. Morris, an Englishman then engaged in making clocks in Grafton," accepted him as an apprentice. It is doubtful if Simon needed much training, for when he was only thirteen he made a striking clock worthy of a master craftsman.

Simon might have been a skillful artisan, but he was no patriot. After serving in the militia for a week, he hired a substitute and returned to Grafton, where he began making wall clocks featuring round brass movements which saved metal. About 1780, Simon moved to Roxbury and marked his shop with a huge double-dial clock. Although he had brought from Grafton some experimental models of a wall clock that would make him internationally famous, Simon spent the first few weeks in Roxbury perfecting a clock-jack—a device for automatically turning a spit used for roasting meat over an open fire—which he had acquired the exclusive right to manufacture in Massachusetts for a period of five years.

Once Simon had completed the necessary work on his clock-jack, he made arrangements with Paul Revere and other leading merchants to act as his agents and resumed his clockmaking activities. An exceptionally skilled workman, Simon needed no pattern when cutting gears out of brass plates with a file and could make a tall clock in six days without help. Eventually, he became so capable with tools—at the age of eighty-five he handled them with the dexterity of a young man—that he could make a shelf or wall clock (without a case) in a single day.

During the winter months Simon made wall clocks ranging in price from ten to one hundred dollars and then, with the coming of Spring traveled about the countryside peddling them. He also fashioned ". . . Time pieces for Astronomical purposes price 70 dollars, Time pieces for meeting houses to place before the gallery, with neat enamelled dials, price 55 dollars. Chime Clocks that will play 6 tunes price 120 dollars." In addition, Simon invented a "perambulator" which could be "affixed to any kind of wheel carriage, and will tell the miles and rods exact, price 15 dollars."

Besides making tall, shelf and wall clocks, Simon manufactured "large Clocks for Steeples" charging $500 for those having one dial, $600 for those having two, $700 for a three-dial clock, and $900 for one with four dials. He constructed tower clocks for many churches, the Old State House

By extending his arm and head through a small opening in its face, a workman repairs the tower clock on the Old State House in Boston, Massachusetts. This clock was made by Simon Willard when he was 78 years old.

in Boston, and other public buildings. In 1801, he made a large clock for the United States Senate chamber, constructing it on entirely new principles, making it necessary for him to go to Washington, D.C., to explain its operation. This clock was destroyed by the British during the War of 1812. While in Washington, Simon became friendly with Thomas Jefferson, who commissioned him to make a turret clock for the University of Virginia. Jefferson, who had a wide knowledge of machinery, gave Simon "the most complete and accurate specifications I have ever received."

Simon's greatest fame rests on the wall clock he completed in the late 1790's and patented in 1802. This "Improved Patent Timepiece" is known to clock collectors as the banjo clock, a name derived from the shape of the case which resembles that of the musical instrument. Both the movement and the case were devised by Simon and authenticated examples of his work carry prices ranging as high as several thousand dollars.

Although Simon frequently had his clocks encased by his nephew, Henry Willard, a well-known Boston cabinetmaker, or by Charles Crehore of nearby Dorchester, the majority of his clocks were sold without cases. However, banjo timepieces were always cased before leaving the shop. A customer had his choice of three different cases, the most expensive being the so-called "presentation case," the ornamentation of which included a glass front decorated with scroll work painted by Charles Bullard, a trained artist.

The banjo sold well and, after 1802, Simon made nothing else. Yet, because his patent was disregarded by other clockmakers, he profited little from his invention. As a result, he refused to patent an alarm clock he devised in 1819. Honest himself and proud of his craftsmanship, Simon ignored the unfair competition and worked in his shop for twelve to fourteen hours a day. During his lifetime he made twelve thousand tall and shelf clocks, four thousand banjo clocks, at least twenty-five tower clocks, and a number of clockwork devices for rotating lamps in lighthouses.

Simon retired in 1838, after selling his tools to his favorite apprentice, Elnathan Taber, to whom he gave permission to place the name Willard on his clocks, if he so desired. Restless in retirement, Simon spent much time in Taber's shop and in the one operated by his son, Simon, Jr., who, after having been graduated from West Point, resigned from the Army and opened an establishment in Boston where he specialized in chronometers. On August 30, 1848, Simon Willard, outstanding craftsman but poor businessman, died at the age of ninety-five.

Aaron Willard, youngest of the Willard brothers, and the only businessman among them, was born in Grafton on October 13, 1757. He probably was trained by one of the many clockmakers in his family and was working in Grafton before the Revolution in which he served for a few years as a fifer.

In 1780, he moved to Roxbury and set up shop near his brother, Simon. The two never seem to have considered working together, although they

LEFT: *Simon Willard's "Improved Patent Timepiece"—known to collectors as the banjo clock (1810).* CENTER: *While Simon Willard was the most famous member of his clockmaking family, his brother, Aaron, Sr., made splendid clocks as shown by this illustration.* RIGHT: *Although Aaron Willard, Jr., made a large number of clocks, his work is avidly sought by collectors.*

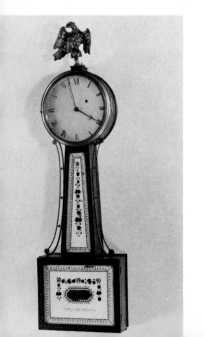

were on friendly terms and both used the services of the same cabinet-makers and other craftsmen who had settled in the neighborhood. Twelve years later, Aaron established himself at 843 Washington Street, Boston, and within a short time was employing thirty workmen who turned out a wide variety of clocks, including those which infringed upon his brother's patent.

After amassing a considerable fortune, Aaron turned his factory-shop over to his son, Aaron, Jr., in 1823. Young Aaron, who invented the lyre-shaped wall clock, carried on the business so successfully that he was able to retire, an extremely wealthy man, at the age of fifty-seven—two years after the death of his father.

While the Willards are among the best known and most expert of American clockmakers, other craftsmen, working during the same period, produced masterpieces of accuracy and design. Lemuel Curtis (1790-1857) not only improved the original banjo clock, but also created the Girandole, a wall clock having a large circular base. Beautifully proportioned and artistically ornamented—the base being painted with a representation of an historical event or a scene from classic literature—the girandole is considered to be the most beautiful clock ever designed by an American.

Meanwhile, in Norwich, Connecticut, Thomas Harland, who had come to America on one of the vessels which carried the tea thrown overboard at the Boston Tea Party, was advertising that he made clocks and watches "in the neatest manner and on the most approved principles." One of the foremost members of his craft in this country, Harland attracted a large number of apprentices, many of whom became famous. Besides his pupils, Harland gave work to a dozen artisans in his shop which turned out brass movements. These were sold to peddlers whose customers bought a case from local cabinetmakers. However, the movement was often left uncased and hung on a wall. Because the exposed swinging pendulum could be seen, such timepieces became known as "wag-on-the-wall" clocks.

Carl W. Dreppard, the antiquarian, once wrote, "Connecticut spells chests, chairs and clocks." While few examples of Connecticut chests are known, there is a plentiful supply of chairs and clocks. There is good reason: both were made by mass-production methods. While Hitchcock is credited with being the first to use factory methods to fabricate chairs, several men played an important part in changing clockmaking from a craft to an industry. Of them all, none was more important than Eli Terry, the first American to make clocks in volume.

Terry was born in East Windsor, Connecticut, on April 13, 1772. Apprenticed to Daniel Burnap, a clockmaker of great skill, Terry not only

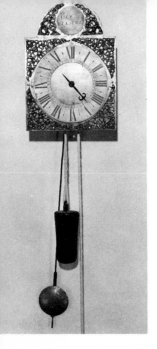

LEFT: *Wag-on-wall clock made by Isaac Blaisdell (1738-1791) of Chester, N.H. Blaisdell not only sold tall clocks but also supplied movements to "people who could not afford the extra expense for the case."* CENTER: *This clock, like all the others made by E. Terry & Sons at their Plymouth, Connecticut, factory, was "warranted if well used."* RIGHT: *Mahogany pillar and scroll clock in an upright case with scroll-carved cresting and two brass urn finials above a white-painted clock face with scene of Mount Vernon beneath.*

learned to make the tools of his chosen craft and clock movements but also the art of engraving brass dials. In 1793, Terry opened his own shop where he made clocks with both brass and wooden movements. Evidently, he was not successful for he also engaged in the selling of spectacles. Hoping to improve himself, he moved to Northbury (now Plymouth), Connecticut, in 1793, but barely managed to make a living. In fact, when he married Eunice Walker in 1795, the couple "are said to have gone housekeeping with only two chairs and two cups and saucers."

Like the other Connecticut clockmakers of his period, Terry drove about the countryside peddling the tall clock movements he had fashioned by hand. Sometimes he found a purchaser who paid the twenty-five dollars he asked for his uncased clocks, but more often he was forced to sell them on the installment plan or exchange them for produce of equal value. Eventually, by shrewd trading, he became very successful.

In 1797, Terry was granted a patent—perhaps the first ever awarded an American clockmaker—for an "Equation clock," which showed the variation between sun and actual time. In the next fifty years he would earn eight other patents as the result of his constant improvement of wooden works clocks which began to replace brass work clocks about 1800.

Wooden movements originated with Connecticut clockmakers who had realized that clocks with brass works were too expensive for the average person. After years of "tinkering," they had succeeded in developing a reliable wooden movement but continued to fashion it by hand. Terry, "the Henry Ford of the early clock business," made the first step toward mass-producing wooden movements in 1800, when, aided by his two employees, he rigged a water wheel in Niagara Brook which ran by his shop and used it to power lathes and saws. Meanwhile, Terry had invented a device for cutting gear-blanks from well-seasoned cherry wood, as well as a machine for forming gear teeth. As a result, Terry and his assistants could make several movements at one time.

In 1807, Terry sold the shop to Herman Clark, an apprentice, and purchased a water-power-driven mill in the town of Greystone. The following year he signed a contract with Levi and Edward Porter of nearby Waterbury for four thousand "hang-up" wooden movements, promising to deliver them within three years. The Porters agreed to furnish the materials and pay four dollars for each movement. To aid him in meeting this contract, Terry formed a partnership with Seth Thomas and Silas Hoadly and, by 1810, the last clock was delivered. That same year Terry sold the Greystone plant to his partners and returned to Plymouth, where he began experimenting in making wooden-movement shelf clocks.

By 1820, he was producing a tremendous number of these clocks, having been granted a patent on his invention in June, 1816. However, unsatisfied

LEFT: *Rare Seth Thomas 30-hour shelf clock with wooden works, having painting on glass of the clock factory at Plymouth, Connecticut, a carved eagle on top, and carved pilasters and feet.* CENTER: *Pillar and scroll shelf clock made by Seth Thomas with painting on glass of Dartmouth College.* RIGHT: *Steeple on steeple clock showing wagon wheel spring invented by Ives.*

with his original movement, Terry was constantly improving it. He also kept changing the shape of the case and is credited by some authorities with designing the style known as pillar and scroll. But other experts claim that Herman Clark originated this rectangular case which has pillars on the front corners and a scroll pattern cut in the top.

No matter who designed it, the pillar and scroll became one of the most popular clock styles ever produced in America, However, Terry did not benefit from introducing it. Not only did his competitors copy the case but also "Terry's Patent" movement, few bothering to pay for the privilege. One exception was Seth Thomas, who paid his former partner a thousand dollars for permission to use the new movement. Thomas' action was most unusual, for, as a rule, clockmakers freely "borrowed" the ideas of others.

By now Terry was making thousands of uncased wooden movements a year for the wholesale trade. Both of his sons, Eli, Jr., and Henry, helped supervise his workmen, as did his brother, Samuel. After Terry, Sr., retired, an extremely wealthy man, in 1834, the others continued to make clocks, both individually and with various partners. It is very difficult to trace their careers, as the Terry family was involved in at least twenty different partnerships.

In his retirement, Terry "turned business into a hobby." He continued to make a few intricately constructed clocks—some with brass works—and to instill tower clocks until his death in Terryville in 1852 at the age of eighty.

Actually, wooden works were an unsatisfactory substitute for brass. The cogs on the gears frequently split, and in damp weather the entire movement had a tendency to swell and stop. Therefore, when rolled sheet brass became available in this country after 1823, clockmakers began using it for movements. They stamped out various parts with machinery and replaced the weights that had powered the earliest clocks with the steel "wagon spring" invented by Joseph Ives. Using assembly line methods, Chauncey Jerome, who had worked with Terry and who had been the partner of P. T. Barnum of circus fame in an unsuccessful clockmaking venture, produced forty thousand brass-works shelf clocks a year.

Not only did Jerome flood the American market, but he also shipped clocks to England. When the first lot arrived, British customs officials thought that Jerome was attempting to avoid paying as much duty as he should by stating that the clocks were worth only eight dollars apiece. Therefore, they seized the shipment under a law that gave them authority to do so after paying the declared value, plus 10 per cent. When Jerome's agent reported what had happened, the clockmaker was delighted—all the shipment had been sold at one time, at a profit, and for cash! He immediately exported a larger consignment, which also was purchased by the British government. However, when a third shipment arrived, the authorities came to the conclusion that Jerome had honestly evaluated his clocks and they were allowed to enter the country in the normal way.

Meanwhile, Seth Thomas, another of Terry's old-time associates, had built a brass rolling mill to supply raw materials for his clockmaking factory which employed nine hundred men. Thomas' two sons, Seth, Jr., and Aaron, expanded the business until it was selling clocks of all types throughout the world. In time, after a series of mergers with other companies, the Thomas concern became part of the present-day General Time Corporation.

While other Connecticut clock manufacturers also mass-produced a wide variety of clocks, many specialized in shelf clocks designed to avoid infringing on Terry's patents. During the first half of the nineteenth century these firms made and sold thousands of clocks. However, no other Connecticut shelf clock was as popular as the O.G.

O.G. (or ogee) clocks derive their name from the molding on their plain, rectangular cases. Used since ancient times, this molding, known as a cyma or ogive curve, consists of a double continuous curve that is concave below, passing into convex above, and is S-shaped in profile. O.G. clocks were made in several different sizes. After 1837, their wood movements were replaced by brass works driven by weights or springs. Although fashions in home furnishings changed through the years, O.G. clocks remained popular for nearly a century, their manufacture stopping just before the outbreak of World War I.

By the 1860's clockmaking was a large-scale industry, some makers

LEFT: *A 30-hour steeple clock made by Chauncey Jerome during his New Haven period, about 1845.* CENTER: *An O.G. clock made by Hotchkiss & Fields, Burlington, Connecticut, about 1840.* RIGHT: *Steeple on steeple clock with eight-day wagon spring power made by Birge and Fuller, Bristol, Connecticut, 1844-1848.*

Blinking-eye clocks.

turning out 100,000 clocks of a popular design a year. Most of them had wood cases, many of them so poorly constructed that an honest cabinet-maker would have destroyed them. Others were skillfully joined. The public by then had the choice of several styles. Among these were the so-called steeple clock—more properly known as the Gothic clock—designed by Elias Ingraham (1805–1885), a leading clock-case designer, and the acorn case, developed by the Forrestville Manufacturing Company, which later became the Sessions Clock Company.

Certain manufacturers began producing cases of cast metal covered with ornamentation about 1870. Today these can be purchased at country auctions for a few dollars. More expensive are the novelty cases made during the same period. They have the form of a human figure and are known as blinking-eye clocks, because the eyes shift from side to side as the pendulum swings.

If Simon Willard could visit a modern clock factory, he would be astonished to see the speed with which complicated machinery fabricates the parts he once so laboriously fashioned by hand. But one thing would not amaze him—the pride owners of old clocks have in their possessions. He and his fellow artisans, true to the traditions of their craft, fashioned their handiwork with honest workmanship, artistic skill, and the best of materials, confident that it would last.

4

Glassmakers

————◁—▷◦◑◈◐◦◁—▷————

No one knows where or when men first manufactured glass. It must have been very early in history, for archeologists have learned that stone beads were glass-glazed in Mesopotamia about twelve thousand years ago. This ancient glass was made from the same materials as most modern glass—sand, lime, and soda.

While these three ingredients are plentiful in the New World, glass-making was unknown to its peoples until the Spanish conquerors of Mexico established a glassworks there in 1535. Yet, long before this date, the Indians of the Western Hemisphere—like all primitive tribesmen—had used glass for weapons and ornaments, although they did not know how to make it. The obsidian they collected in volcanic regions, the quartz they chipped out of sandstone, and other materials from which they formed arrowheads and amulets were "natural glass'—silica which had been fused by intense heat.

The early English colonists soon discovered that the Indians preferred colored glass beads to wampum—the strings of stones and shells they used as money. Tradition holds that such beads were made in the first factory built in what eventually became the United States: a glassworks erected at James Towne, Virginia, in 1608. However, very little glass was made in Virginia or in any of the colonies. Wealthy settlers imported glassware from Europe, while poor people contented themselves with pewter or wooden utensils. Nor was there any great demand for window glass, which was very expensive and subject to high taxation. But even if there had been a market for window glass, it could not have been made in a New World glasshouse—English law forbade factories of any kind in the colonies.

This law—designed to protect English industries—was defied by German-born Caspar Wistar. His opening of a glassworks at Alloway, New Jersey, in 1739, marks the real beginning of glassmaking in this country. A successful manufacturer of brass buttons, Wistar imported four glass blowers from the Netherlands, offering them a share in the profits of his glasshouse in return for teaching him and his son, *but no others,* the secrets of their craft. Originally, Wistar's works made only bottles and a green window

Conjectural reconstruction of the first factory in America, the glassworks at Jamestown, Virginia.

glass but was soon producing glassware of all kinds.

America's first flint glass—a brilliant and clear glass whose formula included lead oxide and sand containing a large proportion of flint—was probably made by Wistar. He also made three-colored glass by fusing one color over another, and was famous for delicate perfume bottles small enough to be carried inside a lady's glove. Martha Washington had one of these bottles, and there is good reason to believe that Benjamin Franklin was also a customer of Wistar for he manufactured, according to an advertisement dated August 17, 1760, "electrifying Globes and Tubes."

Wistar's glassworks was in operation for forty years, closing down during the depression which followed the Revolution. Today, despite the fact that Wistar founded the American glass industry, few know of him except historians and collectors of glass.

On the other hand, William Henry Stiegel's life and works are known to thousands. A colorful, extravagant, romantic individual who assumed the title of "Baron," Stiegel is the most dramatic figure in the history of glassmaking. Like Wistar, he was a German, coming to this country as an indentured servant in 1750 when he was twenty-one years old. Two years later he went to work as a clerk for Jacob Huber of Lancaster County, Pennsylvania, a landowner who had two prize possessions—a daughter Elizabeth and an ironworks.

Stiegel acquired both possessions through marriage. After selling a partnership in the ironworks to the Philadelphia merchants to whom he was originally indentured, Stiegel used the money he received to purchase Charming Forge, another ironmaking plant. Meanwhile, he was active in land speculation and laid out the town of Manheim, Pennsylvania.

Although he owned two furnaces, had founded a town, and accumulated a fortune by buying and selling land, Stiegel—now known throughout the countryside as Baron Stiegel—was constantly in debt. Nevertheless, he lived in luxury in a red-brick mansion on Manheim's Market Square. On the roof of his house, extending between two large chimneys, was a platform on which his private orchestra frequently played. Townsfolk knew when the baron returned home from inspecting his property, even if they didn't see his handsome coach drawn by four sleek horses go by—the booming of a cannon announced his arrival.

Despite the fact that the baron was busy avoiding his creditors, tending to business, giving lavish parties in Philadelphia, or entertaining house

ABOVE: *The rare Stiegel-type amethyst perfume bottle on the left has the daisy-and-button pattern above vertical ribs; the chestnut-shaped flask in the center is olive amber; the Stiegel-type deep amber flask on the right is in an expanded diamond lattice pattern and was made in Ohio.* BELOW: *All of these pieces are blue in color but show wide variation in design. The first is in the expanded diamond pattern; the second is in the same pattern but has an applied flaring foot; the third is classified as "Stiegel type."*

A grouping of early flasks: the sapphire blue flask in the center is flanked by one-half pint enameled flasks, one decorated with an exotic bird and a heart, the other with a cockerel.

guests with balls and masquerades, he did not forget the residents of Manheim. He provided them with a schoolhouse and also deeded a lot to the Zion Lutheran Church. Each year the church pays the rent of the lot to Stiegel's heirs—"one red rose in the month of June, yearly forever hereafter."

But entertaining, education, and lots were expensive and the baron was hopelessly in debt. Seeking some way to pay his bills, he had begun manufacturing bottles and window glass at Manheim in 1765. The venture was so successful that Stiegel built a larger glassworks, but this too had to be enlarged several times. Stiegel eventually employed about 150 workmen, most of whom he brought over from Europe.

Because Stiegel's glassmakers willingly gave him the secrets of their craft, he was able to produce colored glass. The first glass with enameled decorations made in America was fashioned at Manheim, as well as an exceptionally thin crystal glass. Stiegel's plant also made pattern-molded glass—articles whose patterns are molded but not their shape and that have great beauty of line, form, and color. However, the engraving on most Stiegel glass was poorly done.

The baron advertised his wares in every large city and the finest shops stocked his enameled, ribbed, engraved, and colored glassware. Stiegel's account books show that in 1700, over 66,000 pieces of his glass were out on consignment and reveal that he had sold thousands of decanters, jugs, bottles, and candlesticks, and furnished doctors with scientific glassware such as globes, tubes, and retorts.

However, the more money the baron made, the more he spent. His debts became so large that, in order to raise funds, he offered to sell everything he owned except his house and the glassworks. Unable to find a buyer, Stiegel organized a lottery for the benefit of "a Manufactory of public advantage," but the sale of chances netted less than five hundred dollars.

The baron's creditors seized Charming Forge in June, 1773, and six months later took over his Manheim holdings. Late in 1774, Stiegel, the first American to produce table and ornamental glass as attractive in form, color, and decoration as any then being made in Europe, was arrested for debt and thrown into jail. Upon his release, he owned nothing "excepting the Wearing Apparel and bedding for himself and family." It is not definitely known if Stiegel ever returned to Manheim after his imprisonment. Some authorities state he spent his last years as a clerk at Charming Forge and teaching in the school he had founded. Others claim he disappeared during the Revolution. Even the date of the death and the location of the grave of this pioneer American glass manufacturer is unknown.

When the Revolution ended English control of manufacturing in her former colonies, glassworks were built along the east coast and in Ohio. The Federal Census of 1810 lists twenty-two glass factories, but identifying the wares of any one of these glasshouses is practically impossible because early glassmakers drifted from job to job, carrying the techniques of one factory to another.

Most of the glassworks listed in the 1810 census went bankrupt during the War of 1812. It wasn't until about 1820, when a tariff was placed on imported glass by the Federal Government, that the American glass industry was able to compete with European wares. During this period, American glassworks produced a wide variety of glass, including certain bottles that are now eagerly sought by collectors. These bottles, decorated with the images of military and political heroes, historical incidents, the American eagle, and patriotic mottos, made famous the glass factories in

Urn-shaped clear creamer made in Pittsburgh area and an aquamarine "lily-pad" creamer typical of the type produced by the master craftsmen employed in glasshouses in southern New Jersey during the 19th century.

Pittsburgh, upper New York State, New Jersey, Ohio, and the region that was to become West Virginia. But it was in the little village of Sandwich on Cape Cod that the art of glassmaking reached new heights in this country.

Strangely enough, few facts are known about Deming Jarves, the astute businessman and glass expert who founded the Boston & Sandwich Glass Company. The only known picture of him was painted when he was in his seventies; therefore, we have no idea of his appearance during the years he dominated the American glass industry and fashioned wares of great beauty. For that matter, we are not sure when or where Jarves was born. One authority states, "he was born abroad where his parents were travelling" and gives the date as 1791: according to his granddaughter, Jarves was born in 1790. However, we do know the exact date of his death, April 15, 1869.

Son of a Boston cabinetmaker, Jarves went into the drygoods business, became a dealer in crockery, and then, in his mid-twenties, became the sales agent for a group of glass companies. In 1817, Jarves and some businessmen purchased an unsuccessful glass company in nearby East Cambridge which had been managed by Richard Fisher, an English glass cutter who had been smuggled into America in a barrel because it was against British law for a glassworker to leave the country. After reorganizing the firm, Jarves and his associates began manufacturing flint and crown glass—the latter being a good quality window glass.

In order to make flint glass, the New England Glass Company was forced to import lithage or red lead—which, as indicated, is an important ingredient in flint glass—from Europe as none was made in this country. Not only was this expensive, but also, in order to eliminate competition, foreign governments limited the amount of red lead shipped to American glassworks.

Always resourceful, Jarves decided to make his own red lead. All he knew about its manufacture—the process was a closely guarded secret—was that the lithage could not contain the slightest trace of any other metal or it could not be used for making clear glass. Nevertheless, Jarves built an experimental furnace and, to his amazement, succeeded in discovering the secret of obtaining red lead the first time he operated it! For the next thirty years Jarves not only supplied American glassmakers with all the red lead they required but also made red lead for paint manufacturers.

During the next seven years Jarves learned every detail of glassmaking and constantly sought ways to improve the products of the New England Glass Company while, at the same time, lowering costs. Busy as he was, Jarves found time to hold several public offices and probably could have continued to be re-elected if he had so desired, for he "was able to win the

Grouping of early 19th century glass. From left: a barber's bottle made from so-called "end-of-day" glass; a pair of pressed vaseline glass candlesticks in petal and loop design from the Boston & Sandwich Glass Company; and a blown three mold decanter or toilet bottle of sapphire blue glass with a tam o' shanter stopper.

Clear flint glass half-pint decanter, attributed to the Mount Vernon Glassworks, Mount Vernon, New York.

One of the earliest photographs of the Sandwich glass-works, taken with a camera using transparent, flexible rolled film developed by George Eastman, father of popular photography.

LEFT: *Blown three mold decanter and pitcher attributed to the Boston & Sandwich Glass Company. Made about 1830, each piece has a plain base with rough pontil mark, cylindrical body, and sloping shoulder. The decanter has a hollow ribbed stopper molded in a part-size dip mold and expanded.* RIGHT: *This sapphire blue creamer was made by the Boston & Sandwich Glass Company's plant on Cape Cod, but the origin of the gold-flecked bowl is unknown.*

good will of all manner of people without having to buy it with favors."

However, Jarves was not happy at Cambridge. An independent individual, he disliked explaining his plans to associates and much preferred to work alone. Finally, unable to convince his fellow directors of the need to improve the techniques used in the glasshouse and anxious to start a business which could be carried on by his sons, Jarves resigned and formed the Boston & Sandwich Glass Company—which became the most famous glassworks in America during its years of operation.

Jarves chose Sandwich as the site of his factory because the surrounding countryside was thickly wooded, assuring an ample supply of fuel for his furnaces. Jarves secured timber rights to twenty thousand acres and local farmers agreed to cut and haul wood to the glasshouse for fifty cents a cord. Unfortunately, the untold millions of tons of sand piled along the shores of Cape Cod were not suitable for glassmaking. As a result, Jarves used sand from deposits as far away as the West Indies, but eventually got his supplies from pits in Western Massachusetts.

To save time and money, Jarves located his glassworks on a tidal creek so that vessels could be easily loaded with finished glassware after dumping their cargoes of sand close to the furnaces. When Jarves discovered that vessels couldn't use the factory wharf at low tide, he constructed a tramway—a horse-drawn railroad—to carry his freight to and from another wharf. This was probably the first railroad of its kind in the United States.

The building of the tramway was typical of Jarves' ability to find a solution for any problem. In fact, the rapid erection of the Sandwich glassworks was due solely to his personality, enthusiasm, technical knowledge, and business methods. Although proud of his accomplishment, Jarves merely recorded: ". . . ground was broke in April, dwellings for the workmen built, and manufactory completed; and on the fourth day of July, 1825, they commenced blowing glass—three months from breaking ground."

Once production began, Jarves supervised every department, just as he had directed the building of the works. While remaining a perfectionist, he reached decisions quickly and his inventive mind constantly created new techniques to improve the making of glass. Moreover, Jarves had the happy faculty of choosing the right man for the job, but while he allowed him freedom to carry out his assignment, Jarves shared his authority with no one.

Somewhat arrogant in his business dealings, Jarves always insisted upon having his own way. When, in 1848, the factory began producing too much glassware to be taken to market by sailing vessels, Jarves contacted the president of the railroad serving Cape Cod and demanded low rates for his freight shipments. The request was refused.

"If that's the case," Jarves thundered, "I'll build a steamboat to carry my shipments to Boston."

Laughingly, the railroad official replied, "I'm afraid, Jarves, that the acorn hasn't been planted yet that will grow into the oak from which you'll get the lumber you need for your vessel."

Several months later Jarves launched the steamboat *Acorn*. This vessel carried the company's wares to Boston until the railroad met his terms.

At first Jarves operated a single eight-pot furnace, but soon was running four ten-pot furnaces and employing more than five hundred workmen. In 1826, needing more capital, he incorporated the works. He admitted a relative of his wife as one partner, and together they also organized the New England Glass Bottle Company which made black and green glass-wares in Boston and Cambridge for many years. Whenever his new associates disagreed with his plans, Jarves threatened to resign but was always persuaded to remain at his post.

Yet, while Jarves was autocratic, he was one of the first employers to interest himself in the welfare of his workers. The prices at the company store were fair, the rent charged for company-owned houses was low, and Jarves provided for the needy widows of former workmen. He also insisted that the boys who worked for him attend school either in the morning or afternoon, depending upon their shift. This did not please the boys, but the half-dollar Jarves gave each of them to buy fireworks on the Fourth of July did.

Jarves also allowed the boys to make and take home anything they wished from the molten metal remaining in the pots at the end of the working day. He also encouraged his master workmen to experiment and rewarded them for developing new techniques. Jarves, himself, using sand samples from all parts of the world, concocted new mixtures and compounded many formulas for coloring glass.

While most of the individuals who created new techniques or who were outstanding craftsmen at the Sandwich works are unknown, all glass articles decorated with enameled figures produced during the late nineteenth century are wrongly credited to Mary Gregory, one of the company's women employees. Nevertheless, a Mary Gregory did work in the firm's decorating department and there is evidence that she loved children and delighted in portraying them on glassware. A typical piece of so-called Mary Gregory glass will show children playing tennis, blowing bubbles, picking flowers, rolling a hoop, or engaged in a similar activity.

However, Mary Gregory was but one of many women who decorated Sandwich glass, and the clear, colored, transparent, and opaque glass enameled with figures or flowers that now bears her name was made by many glassworks both here and abroad. Actually, the articles they produced were a cheap imitation of a porcelain made by outstanding European artists who received as much as ten thousand dollars for a single vase.

The most famous of all the glassmakers who worked at Sandwich was Nicholas Lutz. Born in St. Louis, a town in the French province of Lorraine, he became an apprentice in a local glassworks when he was ten years old, remaining there until drafted into the French army. Upon being discharged, Lutz emigrated to America and entered the employ of the Sandwich plant in 1869, staying on the job until the glasshouse closed in 1888. Lutz then worked for other glass manufacturers.

Lutz had served his apprenticeship under master workmen in a factory noted for paperweights of exceptional beauty. Many of the weights then made at the *Cristalleries de St. Louis*—and reproduced today by using the original techniques—featured ornamental glass rods known as "cane" because they resemble sticks of Christmas candy. Lutz became an expert at

Sandwich paperweight: an outstanding example of the "dahlia" design—its center contains a rose-colored blossom with blue-and-white stamens and five green leaves on a background of latticinio.

blowing delicate, colorful cane. At Sandwich, using the finest flint glass, he created exquisite candy-cane weights, including those known as millefiori—"many flowers"—because the canes in their centers resemble flowers. Lutz also specialized in paperweights that had glass fruits in the centers, blowing minute apples, cherries, pears, and green leaves on a background of white latticinio—glass crossed and interlaced to form a design. One Lutz paperweight, now a favorite of collectors, contains five strawberries with leaves and blossoms covered with dew resting on a lacy background.

Besides making paperweights, Lutz, using methods originally perfected by early Venetian glassmakers, blew a wide variety of articles of striped glass in which he combined dozens of colors. While this ware was made in many European glasshouses, Lutz was the only artisan to produce it commercially in the United States. He also blew threaded glass which has the appearance of being divided into fine threads. This skilled craftsman, who fashioned some of the most beautiful glass ever made in America, made threaded glass items of all kinds, including engraved pieces. But his colorful miniature glass hats are perhaps the best examples of his skill in the art of threading.

Under Jarves' direction, the Sandwich works turned out everything from toy dishes to cut glass. Yet, although Sandwich produced some excellent cut glass, Jarves' fame rests on his pressed glass. While Jarves always claimed credit for inventing the original glass-pressing machine, the courts awarded the patent to Enoch Robinson of the New England Glass Works. Actually, both men had contrived a device for pressing glass at about the same time and their machines operated in the same way: molten glass was poured into a mold, pressed down with a plunger, allowed to cool and harden for a short time. Then the mold was opened and the finished ware removed.

Jarves may or may not have been the first to invent a glass-pressing machine, but there is no doubt that he improved and speeded up the pressing process. Using two- and three-part molds, he manufactured pressed glass of such excellent quality and design that it looked much like the cut glass being made at the time—some by Jarves himself at the glassworks he had established for his son in South Boston. However, Sandwich pressed glass could be sold more cheaply than cut glass and, as a result, Jarves made plain and colored glassware available to all.

The molds used at Sandwich were made of brass and Jarves designed many of them, including one that would press out articles complete with handles. Perhaps the most famous Sandwich mold was that of a dolphin which was used with great effect to make clear and colored candlesticks. In the 1830's Jarves began making lacy glass—pressed glass with fine

ABOVE: *Once form and design could be achieved by pressing molten gobs of glass in a mold by a plunger, scores of patterns in pressed glass were mass produced. Among the most popular of these was the moon-and-star pattern shown here on part of a dinner service and compotiers.* BELOW: TOP: *Blue opalescent salts at each end are now collector's items, but were in common use before salt shakers became popular. The extremely rare salt in the center was made by the New England Glass Company in East Cambridge, Massachusetts. Known as the Washington and Lafayette salt, it has a bust of each on the sides and the acorn and wild rose pattern on ends.* MIDDLE. *Patriotic motifs were common on cup plates. These are decorated with eagles.* BOTTOM. *A trio of fine cup plates: left, silver-stain ship cup plate; center, eagle cup plate; right, opal ship cup plate.*

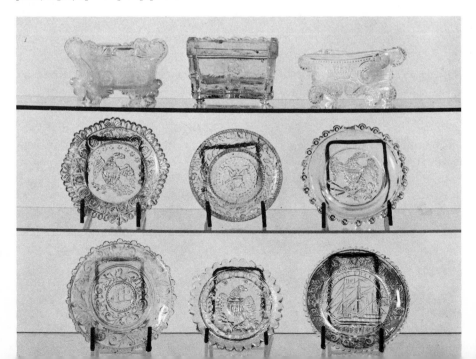

diamond-point backgrounds and lacelike patterns composed of leaves, flowers, peacock feathers, and historical motifs.

While lacy glass is often called "Sandwich glass," this type was also made by other glassworks. Lacy glass is now a collector's item, as is another Jarves' product—the cup plate. This is a small dish in which well-bred people set their tea cups—to avoid staining the table linen—after first pouring the tea into their saucers, from which they drank it. Jarves impressed his cup plates with portraits-in-glass of national heroes and historical scenes. Originally, they sold for five or six cents apiece; today collectors pay large sums for certain types.

For more than thirty years Jarves gave the Sandwich works the benefit of his knowledge of glass and of his business ability. When the local supply of wood ran out, he patented a coal-burning furnace and he also received other patents, some for the improvement of existing devices, others for new machines, including one for making glass knobs. All of his inventions were profitably used at Sandwich until 1858. Then, suddenly, at the age of sixty-eight, Jarves resigned. No one knows why—perhaps he had threatened to leave if he didn't get his way once too often and his associates decided to take him at his word. On the other hand, Jarves still may have been interested in establishing a glassworks which he could leave to his sons, although he had already built a plant for each of them. At any rate, he soon was running another glassworks in Sandwich. When he died, its furnaces were allowed to go out and they were never relighted.

Meanwhile, Sandwich, along with other eastern glasshouses, was finding it difficult to compete with the more modern glass factories which had been established in Pittsburgh, Wheeling, and Chicago. As a result, Sandwich was forced to reduce wages and the workers went on strike. Convinced that their employers were bluffing when they warned that the plant would close if the new wage scale was not accepted, the glassmakers continued the strike. On New Year's Day, 1888, the Boston & Sandwich Glass Company went out of busines.

The closing of the Sandwich works was not the only setback suffered by the glass industry in the East during the 1880's. In the late 1860's William Leighton, a West Virginia glassmaker, had perfected a formula which substituted common lime for the red lead used in the manufacture of flint glass. Unable to learn the secrets of this process and forced to continue to follow the original and more expensive formula for flint glass, eastern glassworks could not produce wares as cheaply as their rivals. Moreover, Pennsylvania and West Virginia glasshouses, closer to the Appalachian coal fields, did not have to pay as much for fuel, which reduced the cost of operation.

This representation of the art of glass blowing in Brooklyn, New York, is believed to have appeared in Harper's Magazine, *probably about 1860.*

Even the New England Glass Company, which had profitably manufactured cut glass during the War Between the States and the subsequent depression, was losing money. In 1878, the nearly bankrupt firm was taken over by its general-manager William Libbey, who had worked for Jarves when he operated the Cambridge plant. In 1883, Libbey died and his son, Edward Libbey, succeeded him.

Young Libbey realized that the only way eastern glassworks could meet the competition of plants in West Virginia and the Midwest was to create new types of glassware. Because it was fashionable to display fancy and colored glass objects on mantelpieces and in cabinets, Libbey decided to specialize in what has become known as "art glass"—well-designed, delicately colored blown and pressed glassware of various kinds. Art glass may have a satin-like finish, be spangled, pebbly, etched, swirled, tooled, or resemble porcelain, to list but a few of its numerous forms.

To assist him, Libbey hired Joseph Locke, an outstanding craftsman specializing in the etching of glass. Locke created Amberina, a bicolored glass with shadings ranging from deep red to pale amber. Fashioned into all types of glassware, Amberina was an instant success.

Prompted by Amberina's popularity, nearly every eastern glasshouse began producing art glass. In South Boston at the Mount Washington Glass Company—the only factory in America where complete crystal chandeliers were made—Frederick Shirley created a translucent glass with colors ranging from an opaque salmon to lemon-yellow. He gave the name Burmese to objects named from this glass and hired well-known artists to decorate his product. Burmese sold well, particularly after Queen Victoria ordered a tea set from Shirley and he publicized the fact.

Perhaps the most famous art glass produced outside of New England is Peachblow. It was first made in Wheeling, West Virginia, following the sale at an auction in New York City of an antique Chinese vase the color of a peach blossom. The original vase cost its purchaser ten thousand dollars, and American homemakers rushed to buy glass imitations of the porcelain masterpiece.

When the demand for novelty glassware dwindled, New England factories again found themselves unable to compete with plants in other parts of the country. Beset by labor troubles and the ever-rising cost of coal, Libbey was forced to close down in 1888—the same year the Sandwich works ceased operations.

However, Libbey continued to manufacture glass. Borrowing money, he went to Toledo, Ohio, where furnaces could be heated by natural gas, and established the Libbey Glass Company in that city. Before long, he was making the finest cut glass that has ever been produced in America.

It is extremely doubtful if cut glass would have become popular in this country were it not for Libbey's showmanship. In order to create a mass

LEFT: *Cobalt blue bowl in expanded ogival (rounded arch) pattern, and a clear blown molded bowl with emerald green banding and foot.* RIGHT: *No other American-made, parti-colored glassware achieved the popularity of Amberina, developed by Joseph Locke, who patented it in 1883.*

market for his sparkling bowls and goblets, Libbey arranged a unique advertisement when plans were made for the Chicago World's Fair of 1893. He secured exclusive rights to manufacture glass at the fair and erected an impressive building on the fair grounds. In the main hall, skilled glassmakers blew glass into various shapes and then, using wheels covered with diamond dust, cut patterns on their surface. But even though Libbey's exhibit was free, the public showed no interest in it. On a hunch, Libbey began charging ten cents for admission. Immediately, the exhibit drew large crowds, and when he raised the price of a ticket to twenty-five cents, the building was thronged!

Although Libbey's display and the souvenir glass hats his craftsmen made at the fair created a demand for cut glass, the expense of the venture nearly made him a bankrupt. Nevertheless, he managed to stay in business and, within a few years, was able to pay off his debts and finance the experiments Michael J. Owens was conducting in hopes of inventing a bottle-making machine.

As a barefoot boy of ten, Owens had been hired by a glassworks in Wheeling, West Virginia, but was told to go home and get his shoes before starting work. Owens had no shoes, but he managed to borrow a pair and entered his apprenticeship. He became a master craftsman, joining Libbey shortly after the opening of the Toledo works, rising to the post of general manager. In 1891, Owens designed a machine that automatically opened and closed glass molds and then began tinkering with a device for mass-producing bottles which were then handmade. They could not be manufactured in a pressing machine as the plunger was unable to pass through their narrow necks. Because bottles were handmade, they were so expensive that druggists insisted that their customers either supply or pay for them when having a prescription filled.

By 1899, Owens had invented a partially automatic bottle-making machine and four years later perfected a fully automatic device operated by compressed air. While Owens' machine made bottles cheap and commonplace, it also changed a handcraft into a mechanical industry. As a result, there was little demand for skilled glass blowers and the art of making decorative glassware was neglected. However, a few craftsmen still employed techniques that were old when Rome ruled the known world to create new types of glass or to create masterpieces from well-known formulas.

Perhaps the best known of these artists-in-glass is Louis Comfort Tiffany, son of the founder of the world-famous jewelry firm. Eccentric, talented, inventive, and versatile, Tiffany was "a man of extravagant fancies and exotic tastes." His own residences—he had four—were lavishly decorated in Oriental style and reflected his love of color.

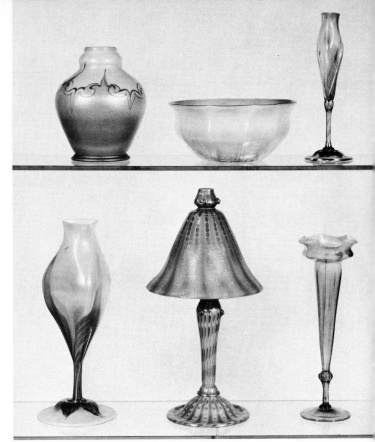

ABOVE: *A grouping of Tiffany glass: leaf-scroll vase; baluster-shaped with lemon-yellow shoulder and banding of pendant leaf scrolls, golden iridescence below on left. Deep bowl in center is mustard yellow at rim to clear, with opalescent white flecking. Floriform vase on right is in iridescent tones of green with three upright leaves, and has a dome foot and collar of leaves.* BELOW: *Examples of Tiffany art glass: the floriform vase on left is same type as one previously described, but larger. Shaded lamp has vertical striations and iridescent golden "beads" and ruffled rim. Right-hand floriform vase is opalescent lemon-yellow at lip; orange to iridescent green at foot and has a ruffled rim.*

After studying painting in Paris and mastering both water colors and oils, Tiffany became interested in the stained-glass windows of European cathedrals. Convinced that he could design and make windows of greater beauty, Tiffany experimented at various glassworks and finally built a "studio" at Corona, Long Island, in 1893. The stained-glass windows he produced there justified his claim that "the best American windows are superior to the best medieval windows."

Although an artist, Tiffany was an excellent businessman and to add to his profits made decorative articles from leftover bits and pieces of the gloriously colored glass he used while fashioning a window. This practice led him into the search for a formula for an iridescent glass and, when he saw that a knowledge of chemistry would make his quest easier, he acquired it. Out of the combination of his study of chemistry, glassmaking skill, and artistic ability came Favrile—an iridescent glass with lustrous colors ranging from deep blue to purple and from green to yellow-gold.

Besides Favrile, Tiffany created several other types of novelty glass, but glassmaking was only one of his interests. He also glazed copper, designed jewelry, molded pottery, worked with textiles, did landscape architecture, and fashioned mosaics. Among the latter is one consisting of nearly a mil-

Lamp, vase, bowl, and jewel box in iridescent shades of green made by Louis Comfort Tiffany in his studio at Corona, Long Island.

lion pieces of Favrile which Tiffany designed for the National Theater in Mexico City. A far simpler example of his work is in the crypt of the Cathedral of St. John the Divine in New York City.

Consecrated to raising the taste of America by making beautiful objects and interesting the public in the decorative arts, Tiffany continued to design and create until his death in 1933 at the age of eighty-five.

While visiting the Paris Exposition in 1900, Frederick Carder, a well-known English glassmaker, saw an exhibit of Tiffany glass and was inspired to create a glass of equal beauty. He named his glass Aurene, because its gold color resembled that of the *aureus*, an ancient Roman gold coin. Carder also made varicolored iridescent glass, fashioning it into tableware and shades for electric-light fixtures. In 1903, Carder came to the United States and established a small glassworks in Corning, New York, calling his plant the Steuben Glass Works. Fifteen years later, he sold out to a thriving glasshouse in the same town—the Corning Glass Works—and became a member of its staff.

In 1933, Arthur Amory Houghton, Jr., the great-grandson of Corning's founder, aided by John M. Gates, an architect, and Sidney Waugh, a sculptor, devised a plan that would enable the Corning works to take full advantage of Carder's technical knowledge and the skill of the workmen he

Using both age-old techniques and modern technology, Steuben artisans today produce beautiful pieces in clearest crystal.

had trained. Houghton's proposal was a simple one. It called for the development of an exceptionally pure and heavy glass from which master craftsmen would fashion both decorative and useful objects designed by outstanding artists. At the same time, Houghton suggested to Corning's board of directors that they re-establish the apprentice system—which had fallen into disuse due to the mechanization of the glass industry—and thus keep alive "the craftsman's historic pride in quality and workmanship."

Houghton's scheme was approved. Today, using both age-old techniques and modern technology, Steuben artisans working with the clearest crystal glass ever made by man produce pieces whose quality, form, and decoration are unequaled in the long history of glassmaking. There is little doubt that in the future their masterpieces—some of which cost several thousand dollars—will be treasured as priceless examples of a supreme contribution to the craft of glassmaking.

5

Porcelain and Pottery Makers

———————⟫•{%•⟨———————

Very early in history man learned that when a basket was smeared with clay it would hold water. It was when such a basket was accidentally left near a fire that our ancestors probably stumbled upon the secret of making pottery. Although we do not know where or when clay was first fashioned into useful articles and then hardened by heat, we do know that the potter's craft is an ancient one, common to all lands.

As the centuries passed, Oriental potters found that if they used a certain clay called kaolin they could produce glasslike, transparent ware. This is now known as china, in honor of the country where it was first made. However, it is equally correct to refer to it as porcelain—the two words are merely different names for the same thing. The famous Venetian traveler Marco Polo is responsible for the word porcelain. Because the bright, white sheen of the vases in the palace of Kubla Khan, emperor of China, reminded him of the shell of the porcellano, a small crab native to the shores of the Mediterranean Sea, he exclaimed "Porcellano!" as he examined the royal treasures.

When European potters—who had no knowledge of kaolin—inspected samples of Chinese porcelain, they were convinced that Oriental craftsmen created it by compounding chemicals in clay. Therefore, they engaged in a wide variety of experiments in hopes of discovering what they thought was a secret formula. Although the potters failed to reproduce the ware imported from the East, they did succeed in manufacturing an artificial porcelain by mixing glass with clay. However, articles made from this substance lacked the beauty of those molded from true porcelain. The experiments continued, but it wasn't until the early eighteenth century when Pere D' Entrecolles, a French Jesuit missionary, smuggled some kaolin out of China that the secret ingredient of porcelain became known.

This knowledge, a horse, the custom of powdering wigs, and a curious chemist paved the way for the establishment of porcelain manufacturing in Europe. The horse belonged to John Schnorr, who noticed it was having trouble lifting its feet. Dismounting, Schnorr examined its hoofs and found

LEFT: *Colonists wanted useful household articles such as this jar and pudding dish made by Hervey Brooks of Goshen, Connecticut, in the early 19th century.* RIGHT: *Examples of late 18th and early 19th century redware.*

that they were covered with a very sticky, extremely adhesive white clay. An astute businessman, Schnorr realized that the clay would make an excellent powder for wigs, and he soon was selling it throughout Germany. Curious as to the composition of Schnorr's product, Johann Friedrich Boettger, a chemist at the court of the elector of Saxony, analyzed it. He found that the powder was pure kaolin.

News of the discovery of kaolin in Germany started a search for this clay in other European countries. Not only were tremendous amounts of kaolin located, but also huge resources of feldspar, another important ingredient in the making of porcelain. As a result, within a very short time, porcelain manufactories were in operation throughout Europe.

But only the wealthy could afford porcelain. Poorer folk had to be content with pottery—sometimes called earthenware—made from local clays. These clays determined the type of pottery in each region (as they still do), but all pottery has a common characteristic: unlike porcelain it is not translucent. Nevertheless, earthenware is often finely made and beautifully decorated, and a joy to behold.

The early American colonists, however, were not interested in either translucence or beauty. All they wanted were useful articles for their kitchens, tables, and dairies. Because their sturdy wooden and pewter tableware has survived and their fragile pottery cups, dishes, and pitchers have disappeared, many people believe that the original settlers of this country used very little pottery for domestic purposes. This is not true. Actually, they used many more pottery vessels in their homes than wooden or pewter ones.

Unfortunately, not only has most seventeenth-century American pottery been destroyed but few records of its production have been preserved. Evidently, the establishment of a pottery was so commonplace that, unlike the opening of a shoemaker's shop, or blacksmith's forge, it was rarely entered in the official records of a settlement. However, we do know that redware—pottery formed from the same type of clay used to make common bricks—was manufactured in Jamestown by 1612 and was also a product of most brickyards operating in the colonies in the early 1600's.

The ware made in brickyards and by such individuals as Dirck Clasen, the "Pott Baker" whose name is listed among the burghers of "Amsterdam, New Netherland" in 1657, consisted of crocks, jars, milk pans, tableware and other simple utensils. As indicated, little of this ware remains except for fragments excavated from colonial kiln sites or from the overgrown cellars of long-vanished homes. Our best source of information about redware is old wills which mention "bowles," "earthen potts," and "juggs."

Philip Drinker, who arrived in Charlestown, Massachusetts, in 1635, is the first New England potter of whom any record exists. Drinker worked with his son, Edward, who carried on the business when his father died. Edward moved his pottery from Charlestown—which had become a center for the craft—in 1663, following his release after arrest and imprisonment for questioning the authority of church officials. Drinker had no competition in Boston and, "after providing its citizens with pots and pans for thirty-five years," died a wealthy man in 1700.

Meanwhile, about 1685, Dr. Daniel Coxe of London, who, although he never came to America, was one of the proprietors and later governor of West New Jersey, had ordered a pottery erected in Burlington, New Jersey, to make "white and chiney ware." While no examples of this pottery exist, it is thought to have been stoneware, an intensely hard variety capable of withstanding extreme heat.

Stoneware was usually decorated with representations of animals, flowers, figures, or geometric designs. The potter used a brush dipped in slip (colored clay of creamy consistency) to incise them. Slip-decorated tableware was also produced by many potters and is most colorful. But the most attractive early ornamented ware is sgraffito, a favorite of Pennsylvania craftsmen. It was made by covering a piece of dry redware with a thin coating of white clay and then scratching a design through it to the red clay below. Often sgraffito wares were glazed with green or yellow oxides before firing, which greatly enhanced their beauty. Glaze, as the word implies, was originally finely ground glass, which, after being mixed with water, was spread over pottery and re-fused by heat. It is used to seal the

ABOVE: *Jug, beanpot, and slip-decorated pie plate by Hervey Brooks.* ABOVE LEFT: *A Pennsylvania Dutch sgraffito plate (early 18th century) bears legend: I have been riding over hill and dale And everywhere have found girls.* CENTER: *Like all sgraffito, this pitcher was covered with slip, a thin batter of clay of a different color, through which the design was scratched before firing.* BELOW: *Typical wares of Lyman and Fenton, Bennington, Vermont.* Top *A cow creamer flanked by two toby jugs.* Bottom *Spouted jug; a book-shaped bottle, and a hound-handled pitcher.*

ware so that it will not absorb liquids.

Although there were several attempts to establish large "china" manufactories in Philadelphia and Boston as early as 1769, they were not successful. However, local potters usually prospered, including one whose name seems too suitable to be true—C. Potts of Norwich, Connecticut.

During the Revolution, most potters, like other colonial craftsmen, took an active part in the fight for freedom. Then they returned to their shops or opened new ones in different locations, as did Captain John Norton. Originally a native of Connecticut, the captain built a small pottery in Bennington, Vermont, in 1793. From this simple beginning, Bennington grew to be a center of the ceramic industry in America.

Norton's grandson, Julius, inherited the pottery, now a large concern, in 1846 and formed a partnership with his brother-in-law, Christopher Webber Fenton, who had been granted a patent on a new type of firebrick. However, because Fenton wished to experiment in many fancy wares and porcelain—there was a large bed of kaolin near Bennington—the partnership was soon dissolved. Nevertheless, Fenton and Norton continued to run separate plants in the same building until 1850, when Fenton built a factory of his own.

While the Norton works continued to produce stoneware by traditional methods until it closed in 1893—after being operated by the same family for one hundred years—Fenton, backed by various partners, made a wide variety of pottery. Actually, Fenton was a better businessman than a potter, although he did receive a patent for coloring glaze in 1849. But his great talent lay in organization and in predicting what the public would buy.

Under Fenton's direction, the United States Pottery Company produced wares ranging from common crockery to bone china. It also made Parian— a porcelain imitation of Parian marble used chiefly to fashion figures—and many novelties: animal figurines, tobies (mugs representing stout men wearing cocked hats which formed the brims), book-shaped bottles, hound-handled pitchers, and cow creamers, in which the mouth was the spout, and the tail, the handle.

Because Fenton hoped to make Bennington as famous for pottery and china as is the Straffordshire district of England, he encouraged his plant superintendent, Decius W. Clark, "a practical genius in every branch of the potter's art," to experiment with various clays and techniques. Moreover, Fenton was the only New England pottery manufacturer of his period to employ molds which enabled him to use mass production methods, although they were in common use in Ohio potteries in the 1840's.

Many Bennington molds were copies or adaptations of English wares, improvised, no doubt, by the workmen Fenton had imported from the British Isles. Among them was Daniel Greatbach, who had modeled designs for other potteries before coming to Bennington where he originated many of the most popular items.

Although the Bennington display was a highlight of the exhibition at the New York Crystal Palace in 1853—winning high praise from Horace Greeley, the famous editor who advised young Americans to seek their fortunes in the West—and the works were enlarged that same year, the company was in financial difficulties. This was due to a combination of overproduction and poor marketing methods. Strangely enough, Fenton, despite his business acumen, did not realize that delicate wares could not be shipped without special packing and, as a result, the amount of breakage was tremendous. Finally, when he did introduce proper packing procedures, the cost was prohibitive.

The Bennington works closed in May, 1858. Most of the workmen had been unpaid for months, but Fenton gradually settled their accounts. He then moved to Peoria, Illinois, where, in 1859, he started a pottery with his former superintendent from Bennington, Decius W. Clark, but the venture was a failure. Six years later Fenton died.

About that time Captain Norton fired the first kiln at Bennington, a pottery shop was established in Philadelphia's Sugar Lane by Andrew Miller, who passed the secrets of the craft on to his son, Abraham. Young Miller became one of the country's leading potters and during his career contributed greatly to the development of the ceramic industry.

Abraham Miller was a man of many talents. Interested in politics, he served as a member of the state senate and distinguished himself as an advocate of social reforms. He also was active in promoting the Franklin Institute in Philadelphia, the oldest organization in America devoted to the study of the mechanical and applied sciences.

At the Institute's exhibition in 1824, Miller displayed a silver luster

A luster ware pitcher.

pitcher—making him the first American potter to produce luster ware. Originating in the Orient and introduced into Spain by the Moors in the ninth century, the technique of giving clay articles the luster of metal was a closely guarded secret, but gradually became known throughout Europe. It consisted of glazing the clay with metallic oxides of gold or platinum. The latter was used to give the clay a silver coating, while gold was employed to give metallic effects ranging from deep bronze to pink and purple.

Miller's display at the exhibition of 1835 also won great praise. It showed all the stages of pottery manufacture, from raw materials to the finished ware. Even more impressive was the collection of his handiwork which Miller presented to the public in 1842. The handsomely decorated tableware, ornamental vases, and fancy flower pots demonstrated the variety of his production.

However, most of Miller's pottery was simply designed earthenware of various types, although his most popular creation was a pottery mug which depicted Robert Burns's famous character Tam O' Shanter. While Miller made a considerable amount of porcelain, he never offered any for sale. Nor did he market the figures he modeled from white clay. An outstanding modeler, Miller delighted in using "lace-work" on his figures. After soaking a piece of lace in white slip, he placed it in position, then fired the figure. The heat of the kiln destroyed the lace, but the clay retained its original shape.

Before Abraham Miller died in 1858, he had witnessed great changes in pottery making. Not only were Americans producing porcelain equal to any made in England, but the utilitarian and fancy wares of the large potteries which had been established in such centers as East Liverpool, Ohio, and Trenton, New Jersey, had ended the era of the independent local pottery. However, in the so-called "art potteries" and in isolated regions, craftsmen still fashioned clay by hand—as they do today.

Following the War Between the States, potteries were established in many parts of the United States, some specializing in commercial wares, others in decorative art pieces. While the majority of these plants are unknown today except to collectors, a few are still operating. Of the latter, none has had a more fascinating history than Lenox Incorporated.

Walter Scott Lenox, founder of the firm, was born in Trenton, New Jersey, in 1859. As a boy he became interested in pottery and, when not attending school or helping in the family hardware store, modeled clay which he decorated after having it baked in a nearby kiln. Soon he was using a vacant room above the store as a studio where he ornamented ware for local potters.

Most of these wares were crude, but Lenox didn't realize how coarse they were until the day he visited a friend and was served tea in a dainty cup with a luster that resembled mother-of-pearl. Tactfully inquiring where the cup was made, he learned it was of Irish manufacture and was called Belleek. From that moment, Lenox was determined to create a china of equal beauty.

A short time later he became an apprentice in the Ott & Brewer pottery where William Bromley, Jr., son of the manager of the Belleek works, was employed. When the making of Belleek was temporarily suspended in Ireland—today, the ware is one of that country's most valuable exports—Bromley suggested that his father be offered a job in Trenton. He was, and he accepted. He was accompanied by several of his best workmen and upon their arrival and thanks to their knowledge, Ott & Brewer began producing an exquisite, ivory-colored Belleek.

After learning the techniques of the Irish craftsmen, Lenox joined the staff of the Willets Pottery where eggshell china was being developed. Appointed head of the decorating department, Lenox became a close friend of Jonathan Coxon, the English-trained superintendent of the works. In 1889, the two formed their own pottery company.

However, financing their venture was difficult. Lenox did not have any money and the long list of china manufacturers who had failed gave the bankers of Trenton an excuse to refuse to grant him a loan. Finally, William Hancock, a friend, lent Lenox enough money to build a block-square building. Shrewdly, Hancock protected his investment by insisting upon supervising the construction of the building and designed it so that he could convert it into an apartment house if necessary.

This Lenox coffee service is the only American china on exhibit at the Ceramics Museum at Sevres, France.

LEFT: *A collector's item, this Lenox plate was handpainted by William Morley, a craftsman who died in 1934.* RIGHT: *Lenox on display at the Metropolitan Museum of Art, New York. These special exhibit plates cost $18,000 a dozen.*

By 1896, Lenox was able to buy out Coxon, but he was always in debt. In fact, much of his time was spent in borrowing from one friend in order to pay back a loan given by another. Meanwhile, Harry A. Brown, secretary of the company, frequently seized an assortment of ware as it was taken from the kilns and rushed it to New York City, sold it, and bought sorely needed materials for another batch with the money he had received.

Just when the firm's "American Belleek" was selling well enough to make maneuvering unnecessary, Lenox, at the age of thirty-six, was stricken with locomotor ataxia. However, although paralyzed and almost blind, he continued to go to his office every day for the next twenty-five years, being carried to his desk by his chauffeur. Alert in mind, he directed operations, "seeing" what had to be done through the eyes of Harry A. Brown.

In 1919, Brown was able to announce that, at long last, the company was out of debt. To celebrate, a miniature kiln was brought into Lenox's office and all the notes and mortgages were burned in it. But Walter Scott Lenox did not live to see his company grow into a multimillion dollar corporation—worn out from years of struggling with his handicaps, he died on January 11, 1920.

Since its founder's death, Lenox has continued to make fine china. While modern methods are employed to produce the "body" of the firm's wares, the traditional techniques of the potter are employed for "command performances"—special orders from museums, royalty, and heads of state. In some instances Lenox has received as much as a thousand dollars for a handcrafted plate made of lustrous, translucent china ornamented with rich gold work and flowing colors. These creations, along with the company's conventional china, have little in common with the redware of colonial days. However, both are examples of the potter's pride in his ancient craft.

6

Workers in Precious Metals

Gold and silver have been fashioned into articles of great beauty for countless centuries. However, because it is heavier than silver, gold is not only more difficult to work but also impractical for many purposes. Therefore, silver has long been the preferred choice of those who fabricate ceremonial objects and household wares from precious metals. Actually, goldsmithing and silversmithing are one craft, as they employ the same techniques. In fact, until recently, "goldsmith" meant a craftsman who worked in both gold and silver.

The smithing of silver reached its highest peak in England, and the practices of craftsmen in that country spread to the New World. As a result, the first silverwork done in America reproduced articles made in Europe. However, colonial silversmiths gradually developed styles of their own, but their handiwork—which features a fine sense of proportion—was never as ornately decorated as English silver.

A silversmith required more skill and artistic ability than other metal workers. The intrinsic value of his material made careful workmanship mandatory and inspired him to create objects of lasting beauty. Moreover, unlike other smiths, the silversmith had to have the absolute confidence of the public, for in the seventeenth and eighteenth centuries every piece of silver was made to order—the customers furnishing the metal in the form of coins.

Not all these coins came from England. Merchants, sea captains, and innkeepers could easily accumulate a large number of French and Spanish coins which were accepted in the colonies because of the shortage of currency. However, many of these coins had a low silver content. English coins, on the other hand, contained a high proportion of silver. Their quality was set by a law which required then to be "sterling." This term is derived from "Easterlings," the name a group of German immigrant silversmiths working in England gave themselves because their homeland lay to the East. About 1300, King John commanded these craftsmen to refine the silver in the royal treasury and fabricate it into coins. Then, in 1343, an

An early American teaspoon, made by William Moulton, Newburyport, Massachusetts, before 1793.

official degree dropped the first two letters from "Easterling" and established "sterling" as the term to identify silver of the same standard as that made for the king—925 parts of silver to 1000 parts of metal.

If a client's coins were not of sterling quality, the silversmith removed the excess base metal by a chemical process. Members of the craft had to be men of honor, for they could easily claim that the coins given them were low in silver content. However, silversmiths rarely betrayed the trust placed in them.

Actually, a silversmith took the place of a modern banker. Realizing that stolen silver coins could not be identified, the wealthy insured themselves from loss by commissioning the making of silverware, which, even if it did not bear their initials or coat-of-arms, would be stamped with the maker's name. Therefore, when a thief was caught, the silversmith would recognize his handiwork and show that he had a record of the order, thus making it possible to claim ownership. Moreover, the silversmith's skill was comparable to interest—it added to the original value of the silver.

About 1750, silversmiths began supplying their own silver, adding its cost to the fee they charged for fashioning it into other forms. Nevertheless, they continued to melt down coins—particularly those from the Spanish colonies in South America—because silver was not successfully mined in the United States until 1852.

After melting down the coins and removing any excess base metal, the silversmith cast the molten mass into a flat sheet called a "plate." These castings differed in thickness, size, and shape, according to the type of article the craftsman planned to make. The next step was "raising" the

Note the identifying marks on this early American skewer.

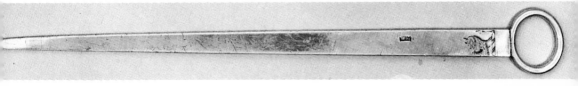

An example of repoussé *ornamentation, this silver tea and coffee service, bearing the imprint "Bailey & Co. Phila. 1830," has beaded rims above key-fret banding, as well as the* repoussé *floral design.*

metal—hammering the flat plate into definite form—by means of variously shaped mallets and anvils. Because silver has a tendency to become brittle when pounded, the smith constantly reheated the metal to a temperature just below its melting point, then cooled it slowly. This process which prevents brittleness is technically known as annealing.

It is no easy task to draw silver into a definite shape, as it has a tendency to spread in one direction when pounded. Therefore, nothing the silversmith did required greater skill than "dragging" his material into the desired shape. Once this was accomplished, the craftsman could solder legs, spouts, or handles into place.

Silverwork was ornamented in three ways: embossing, engraving, or separately cut. The first method—also known as *repoussé*—consists of placing a raised design on an article. Because it is difficult to work from the reverse side of a design when embossing hollow ware such as cups, mugs, pitchers, and teapots, early craftsmen filled such articles with pitch, then hammered the ornamentation in outline from the outside with dull chisels.

While this "flat chasing" was often the only embossing a piece received, frequently it was merely the first step. After the design was outlined, the smith removed the pitch and went to work with snarling irons—so-named because of the sound they make when struck.

One end of a snarling iron was curved and fashioned into a die. Choosing the iron that would create the particular design he desired, the silversmith would fasten it in a vise, setting the curved end inside the piece at the point he wished to push outward. By striking the opposite end with a hammer, the smith raised the decoration on the metal.

Engraving was a far simpler process, the metal being cut away in thin lines with a sharp tool. Silver engraving demanded great skill and, because the process was very similar to that used to engrave illustrative material on copperplates, silversmiths were often asked to make pictures for books and to fashion plates for seals and paper money.

Two different techniques were used to ornament silver by the separately cut method. The first consisted of carving a wooden pattern of the decoration and inserting it in wet sand. When the pattern was removed the smith poured molten metal into the cavity, and, after the casting cooled, it was smoothed with files and soldered into place. The second technique was to cut the decorations from a thin sheet of silver, rather than casting them.

The earliest known American silversmith is John Mansfield, who migrated from London to Boston in 1634. Other English-trained silversmiths settled in the Massachusetts Bay Colony. Among these was Robert Sanderson (1608-1693), who formed a partnership with John Hull (1624-1683).

An engraved bowl made by Ebenezer Moulton (1768-1824) of Newburyport and Boston.

Early American silver porringers.

Silver pitchers by Ebenezer Moulton, the one on the right presented to Isaac Harris in 1810 after he saved the Old South Church from burning. BELOW: *Large spoon made by Jacob Hurd, small one by Benjamin Burt.*

Hull was probably the first silversmith to learn his craft in the colonies, having been apprenticed to his half-brother, Richard Stover, a member of the Goldsmith's Guild of London.

Hull recorded in his diary that after coming to Boston as a boy, he "fell to learning (by the help of my brother) and to practising the trade of a goldsmith, and, through Gods help, obtained that ability in it, as I was able to get my living by it." Hull evidently made an excellent living for he was recognized as a master craftsman. In 1652, he was appointed mintmaster of the Massachusetts Bay Colony and, with his partner, began the coinage of the famous pine-tree shillings. The die for these coins was made by Joseph Jenks at his ironworks near Lynn, and Hull continued to use it until his death; thus, every coin bore the same date, 1652. Because Hull and Sanderson received one shilling out of every twenty they coined, both became wealthy. Of the two, Hull accumulated the larger fortune as he was active in the West Indian trade. Few fathers in colonial days gave their children as expensive a wedding gift as Hull presented to his daughter—he placed the bride on one pan of a set of scales and piled sacks of pine-tree shillings in the other pan until both hung even!

Besides minting coins, Hull and Sanderson made spoons, which differed in shape from those in use today; porringers (small bowls with a flat handle set flush to the rim, the handles being ornamented with openwork designs); various drinking vessels, including cups with and without handles for both household and religious use; and church and domestic silver. They also made "great-salts"—a container which was placed at the right elbow of the host and the left elbow of the guest of honor—individual salt-and-pepper shakers not becoming common until the late eighteenth century.

In 1659, Hull accepted Jeremiah Dummer (1645-1718) as an apprentice, writing in his diary, "The Lord make me faithful in the discharge of this new trust committed to me." Dummer must have been well trained, for he became an outstanding silversmith who characteristically decorated his handiwork with a fluted band. One of Dummer's apprentices was his future brother-in-law John Coney (1655-1722), who also became a leading silversmith. Not only did Coney use his initials to identify his products but also a rabbit—a pun on his name, as "coney" is an old term for rabbit. In addition to working as a silversmith, Coney was also an engraver. He made the plates for the first paper money issued in the colonies and the first seal for Harvard College.

The list of these talented American silversmiths of the seventeenth and eighteenth centuries is a long one. Boston craftsmen included Edward Winslow; Timothy Dwight; John Burt and his sons, William, Samuel, and Benjamin; Jacob Hurd, who made the only New England teapot now known, his son Benjamin, and his son Nathaniel, who was more famous for

93

engraving bookplates than silver, although he was a highly skilled silversmith. In New York City, Cornelius van der Burch, Bartholomew Schaats, Simeon Soumain, Cornelius Kierstede, the Le Roux family, and Myer Myers, a Jewish silversmith who fashioned ritual silver for both Protestants and his co-religionists, among others, produced wares of great beauty.

The thriving seaport towns of Rhode Island supported several silversmiths, the best known being Samuel Vernon of Newport, and James Gorham of Providence, whose descendants were to expand the business he founded into a major silver manufactory. But of all Rhode Island silversmiths, none is more celebrated than Samuel Casey of Little Rest. Casey combined unusual artistic skill with a talent for counterfeiting. Caught, convicted, and condemned to hang, Casey, assisted by friends, escaped from jail, never to be heard of again.

Silversmiths also worked in Southern cities. While John Brodnax is the earliest known craftsman to operate a shop in Virginia, William Callicut, "refyner," arrived in Jamestown in 1608. Other smiths operated shops in Charleston, South Carolina; Baltimore, Maryland; and elsewhere; but none of these were very successful, because plantation owners preferred to import silverwork from England.

Silver ecclesiastical goblets and flagons presented to the Second Church of West Newbury, Massachusetts, by individual parishioners in 1822.

Philadelphia silversmiths fashioned thousands of "Peace Medals" for presentation to friendly Indians.

GEORGE WASHINGTON
PRESIDENT 1793

On the other hand, Philadelphia silversmiths prospered. Philip Syng, Sr., an Irish-trained goldsmith, taught his sons, Philip, Jr., John, and Daniel, his craft before establishing himself in Annapolis, Maryland. Philip, Jr., became a close friend of Benjamin Franklin and a co-founder of the University of Pennsylvania. Working with his fellow silversmiths, Joseph Richardson and William Hollingshead, Syng helped fashion more than eight thousand silver ornaments for use by Indian traders. Richardson also made "Peace Medals" given to friendly Indians. Syng's best-known creation is the silver standish—a stand for holding ink, sand, and quill pens—which was used by the Signers of the Declaration of Independence.

America's most famous silversmith is Paul Revere, who was equally skilled as a coppersmith, goldsmith, and founder of brass and iron. Revere also manufactured cannons, church bells, and copper sheathing. Moreover, he engraved and printed political cartoons; made seals; did blacksmithing; and fashioned and fitted false teeth "as well as any Surgeon-Dentist who ever came from London."

As a lad of thirteen, Revere's father had migrated to Boston from the Island of Guernsey, to which his family had fled from France seeking religious freedom. Arriving in the New World without his parents, the boy apprenticed himself to John Coney, became a fine craftsman, married, then opened his own shop in 1723. At the same time he changed his name from Appollos De Rivoire to Paul Revere, because, as his son later explained, ". . . the Bumpkins could pronounce it easier."

Paul, who was born January 1, 1735, was taught silversmithing by his father. He showed great talent and when the elder Revere died in 1754,

95

A grouping of Paul Revere spoons. Note the wear on center spoon, probably caused by teething of a child.

although but nineteen, Paul was capable of carrying on the business. Two years later he laid down his tools, joined an artillery regiment as an officer, and marched off to fight the French. Upon his return, he reopened the shop and became a respected silversmith.

Revere's silverware is distinguished not only for its workmanship but also for its beauty of design and its wide variety of form. Graceful of line and with fine proportions, his handiwork is often sumptuously decorated, because his clients demanded that their silver be ornamented with crests, initials, inscriptions, or embossing.

In satisfying his customers, Revere developed great engraving skill and this led to experimentation in copperplating. In 1765, he engraved the scores of *A Collection of Psalm Tunes* and soon was engaged in making engravings for books, newspapers, and bookplates. He also fashioned copperplate engravings of Boston Harbor, Harvard College, and prominent men, as well as the plates for many seals, including that of Philips Andover Academy.

An active member of the Sons of Liberty—an organization of colonists who wished to win freedom from England—Revere used his engraving talent to make copperplate cartoons ridiculing the British authorities. His most famous political engraving, published in 1770, is a picture of the Boston Massacre accompanied by a patriotic verse.

As a leader in the revolutionary movement, Revere took part in the Boston Tea Party. An excellent horseman, he was made messenger for the

Committee of Safety, riding as far as Philadelphia with secret reports as well as taking his famous "midnight ride" to warn the Minute Men that the British were coming.

During the Revolution, Revere neglected his shop and devoted himself to military activities. In November, 1775, he was sent to Philadelphia to inspect a powder plant in order to gather the information that would make it possible for him to construct a similar works near Boston. The owner of the mill refused to let Revere take notes or make drawings, so he memorized all the necessary details and built a duplicate plant in Canton, Massachusetts, the following February.

The year 1775 was a busy one for Revere, craftsman and patriot. Authorized to design the first national paper money issued by the Continental Congress, he not only engraved the plates but also constructed the presses to print the money. Because of the scarcity of copper, Revere was forced to engrave the bills on the back of half of his copperplate of Harvard College, and he had great difficulty accumulating enough metal for plates when he was commissioned to design and print paper money and a seal for Massachusetts.

Meanwhile, Revere was manufacturing cannon for the colonial army, repairing the cannon the British had spiked before evacuating Boston, and carrying out his duties as lieutenant-colonel in the Massachusetts artillery. Falsely accused of cowardice in 1779, he was acquitted by a court-martial in 1792, but the verdict came too late to allow him to achieve his ambition of securing an important post in the Federal Government. However, his

LEFT: *The picture that sparked a revolution—Paul Revere's copperplate engraving of the Boston Massacre.* RIGHT: *Paul Revere's business card.*

reputation as a craftsman did not suffer and, in 1780, he was asked to engrave a new Massachusetts seal.

Besides filling orders to fashion silver, Revere opened a store where he sold copper, brass, silver, and gold articles, many of which he made himself, with the assistance of his son, Paul, who was to become an excellent silversmith, too. Revere also established a brass and iron foundry. Another son, Joseph Warren Revere—named for Revere's good friend the soldier-doctor who fell at Bunker Hill—assisted him in the venture. The Reveres cast church bells and were the suppliers of the ironwork and cannon for the *U.S. Constitution*, better known as "Old Ironsides."

In 1801, Revere built a copper rolling mill at Canton, and from it came products used by the United States Navy and private customers. In time, the mill developed into one of America's industrial giants—Revere Copper and Brass Incorporated.

Revere continued his busy career until his death on May 10, 1818, at the age of eighty-four. Although he had achieved success in many fields, his name would stand high on the list of American craftsmen if he had only designed, fashioned, and engraved the punch bowl ordered by the "Fifteen Sons of Liberty" in 1768. Authorities agree that in creating this bowl—the most famous piece of American silver, now displayed in Boston's Museum of Fine Arts—Paul Revere reached "a degree of excellence rarely attained by any other silversmith."

Like furniture, the wares made by silversmiths reflect the ever-changing taste of the public. Silverwork of the colonial period is simple in form and ornament—although there is considerable decoration on pieces made in New York City where the traditions of Dutch silversmithing prevailed. From 1697-1720—"The High Standard Period"—customers demanded fluting, gadrooning, and cast ornamentation of their silver. By the middle of the eighteenth century, ornate decoration was the current fashion—beaded moldings and festoons of flowers and foliage. During this period craftsmen placed elaborate finials on the various shaped lids of teapots and sugar bowls and often supplied a small footed tray for such articles to rest upon. Philadelphia silversmiths pleased their customers by placing a pierced railing on much of their hollow ware which was now made by rolling silver into thin sheets and hammering it into shape.

Actually, much of this silver is over-decorated, although a considerable amount of the work of later silversmiths is most attractive. However, by 1850, the era of the silversmith was coming to an end. A few craftsmen, working with coin silver—an alloy composed of silver mixed with 10 per cent of copper—still operated shops, but were finding it difficult to compete with silver pieces mass produced in factories.

ABOVE: *The most famous piece of American silver—the Liberty Bowl made by Paul Revere.* LEFT: *The simple beauty of a colonial beaker. By Ebenezer Moulton.*

The decline of silversmithing began in 1742, when Thomas Bouslover of Sheffield, England, accidentally discovered, while repairing a knife, that he could fuse a thin sheet of silver to a thicker sheet of copper and that the combination could be treated as a single metal. While Bouslover did not profit from his discovery, others did, and tremendous quantities of so-called Sheffield plate were manufactured. Then, when after a series of experiments in their Hartford, Connecticut, shop, William, Asa, and Simeon Rogers perfected a method—based on an English process—of plating silver electrochemically—Sheffield was priced out of the market.

However, despite mass production, a set of sterling silver—although factory made—is still desired by nearly every housewife. Meanwhile, the ancient craft of silversmithing is being carried on by a few individuals. It is entirely possible that their creations will someday be sought by collectors. But it is extremely doubtful that any of their handiwork will fetch the amount of money paid recently for a tankard made by Paul Revere—thirty thousand dollars!

99

7

Pewterers

Man must have discovered how to make pewter about the same time he learned to fabricate bronze, for both are alloys of tin and copper. Various objects made by ancient peoples indicate that they compounded pewter by combining nine parts of tin with one part of copper—the same formula in reverse ratio (nine parts of copper and one of tin) being used to make bronze. In time, as pewter became more widely used and the pewterer's craft grew in importance in Europe, the original formula underwent refinements. Actually, there were almost as many formulas for making this gray-hued silvery metal as there were pewterers. Craftsmen added antimony and bismuth to toughen, harden, and temper the tin, and introduced lead to make their alloy more malleable.

Not only did lead make pewter easier to work, but also it was cheaper than tin. Therefore, certain pewterers placed large amounts of lead in their mixture. As a result, their wares were dark, soft, and easily dented, and did not shine as did articles containing a larger proportion of tin.

Proud of their craft and anxious to protect the public from unscrupulous artisans whose handiwork contained a high lead content, the pewterers of London secured a charter from Edward IV in 1473 which gave the "Craft of Pewterers" the right to assay all pewter brought to London, to search the shops of English pewterers, and to seize any pewterware of sub-standard quality.

By constant supervision the Worshipful Company of Pewterers—which still maintains a Guildhall in London—protected the public from inferior merchandise. To show that they guaranteed the quality of their metal and workmanship, master craftsmen used a special tool to place a "touch mark" on their products. Each pewterer had his own touch, which was registered with the Guild. However, the right to use these trademarks was granted only after an artisan had submitted a sample of his work for approval.

In America, neither was there a guild to regulate the craft, nor rules about marking. Nevertheless, the best pewterers followed the practices of honest English craftsmen. But since there was no regulation requiring marking, many did not use touch marks.

The average early American colonist would have been proud to own pewterware with or without a touch mark, even if it was made of "lay metal" (tin and lead), for only the wealthy could afford pewter. Nevertheless, as early as 1629, pewter "botles of pyntes and qrts" were being imported from England and, by 1654, Thomas Bumpsteed was successfully operating a pewter shop in Boston. In time, that city became the center for the distribution of pewter throughout the colonies, and consignments of pewter spoons, pans, pots, tankards, "basons," and "sawcers" were shipped there.

Actually, the individuals who are listed as pewterers in colonial records of the seventeenth and eighteenth centuries were primarily dealers in English pewterware. Because of trade restrictions it was impossible for them to secure tin from Europe, so the only opportunity they had to practice their craft was to repair broken articles or to cast them into new forms. Besides casting old pewter, they hand-hammered it into new objects or turned it on a lathe to create utensils—frequently combining all these techniques.

Because much colonial pewter was melted down into bullets during the Revolution, no identifiable specimens of the work of the earliest American pewterers exist. Moreover, no known pieces of American pewter made before 1750 bears the name of its maker. Colonial pewterers, fearful of having their work compared with that of English craftsmen, deliberately refrained from using a touch mark.

Nevertheless, we do know the name of a few pewterers who were work-

LEFT: *An example of a pewterer's touchmark, a ship and the words "Success to the United States of America" appear inside a tankard. This piece was probably made in Scotland for export.* RIGHT: *Pewter whale oil lamp with saucer base, baluster stem, cylindrical reservoir, and loop handle. Marked "R. Gleason," an early 19th century pewterer in Dorchester, Massachusetts.*

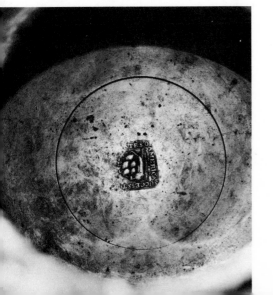

ABOVE: *Early pewter—chargers, eight-inch-plates, inkstand, and beaker.* BELOW: *Outstanding pewterers fashioned these articles—Nathaniel Austin made the charger; Thomas Danforth the "bason"; while the pitchers—from left to right—are the work of F. Porter, Roswell Gleason, and Joseph Danforth, respectively.*

ing here before 1750. In Boston, Thomas Bumpsteed, Henry Shrimpton, John Comer, Thomas Clark, and Samuel Green dealt in pewterware; as did William Horsewell and John Holden in New York City; while Simon Edgell and James Everett had shops in Philadelphia. Little is known of these men. In fact, the only pewterer of this period of whom we have any detailed information is Richard Graves of Salem, Massachusetts, However, it is not Grave's pewtering skill that makes him famous, but his criminal record!

Not only was Graves accused of neglecting his duties as a ferryman by the authorities, but also he was sentenced to sit in the stocks for beating a neighbor, whipped for kissing "Goody Gent twice," and fined for stealing wood and fence rails. In addition, Graves got into difficulties over the ownership of some molds and for "playing at shuffle-board, a wicked game of chance."

However, the majority of pewterers, like most colonial craftsmen, were respectable citizens. With more raw material available, they became valued members of their communities, furnishing buckles, buttons, candlesticks, chandeliers, coffee and teapots, Communion services, drinking vessels, dishes, flatware, and other articles. A considerable number of pewterers became successful businessmen and gave up craftsmanship for trade or banking. Among those was Henry Shrimpton. He was so proud of his pewtering skill that, when he retired, he placed a large pewter teapot on the roof of his house to indicate the source of his wealth.

Because the eight-inch dinner plate was the size most commonly fashioned by pewterers between 1750 and 1825, the craftsmen of that period are known as the "Eight-Inch-Plate-Men." Actually, of all the pewterers who operated shops during this span of seventy-five years and whose marked work is known, only two did not make such plates.

One of these is George Coldwell, "pewter spoon and candle mold maker" of New York City, who did his best work between 1792 and 1796. Coldwell is the only known specialist among early American pewterers. He is also famous for placing his name on his spoons. Usually pewter spoons were cast or repaired by householders who owned a spoon mold, A Colonel William Will, who served as a member of the Pennsylvania Assembly when he wasn't keeping an inn or pewtering, also made table and teaspoons which he marked with a touch.

Some of the most famous American pewterers were "Eight-Inch-Plate-Men." Among them are Gershom Jones of Boston, Francis Bassett of New York City (some authorities consider his work the most valuable of all American pewter), and Samuel Hamlin. The latter is one of the craftsmen who made the wares that were produced in Providence and Newport, Rhode Island, so distinctive. Hamlin has another claim to fame. He alone

—with the exception of George Coldwell—of all known pewterers of this era never made an eight-inch plate.

But no American pewterer is better known than Thomas Danforth of Taunton, Massachusetts, and Norwich, Connecticut. Not only is he one of the earliest pewterers whose work has survived, but also he founded a dynasty of craftsmen whose shops furnished pewterers for nearly a century. Born in Taunton in 1703, Danforth moved his shop to Norwich in 1733, working at his craft until his retirement in 1773.

Danforth, his descendants, and Danforth-trained apprentices dominated the American pewter trade. In fact, the majority of known marked pewter is their handiwork. Besides turning out tremendous amounts of pewter, members of the Danforth school were also outstanding merchandisers, employing peddlers to dispose of their wares, consisting, for the most part, of items for which there was a steady demand. Actually, few of the Danforths were expert craftsmen and most of their work is run-of-the-mold, displaying little originality of form.

Nevertheless, by aggressive salesmanship they established an ever-growing market for their wares. Because there were too many Danforths and Danforth-trained pewterers in Norwich, some of the family and its pupils opened shops elsewhere. Several remained in Connecticut—as early as 1750, Thomas Danforth II and Jacob Whitmore were operating in Middletown. Others settled in Hartford and Meriden, while Samuel Hamlin, who had been a Danforth apprentice, went to Providence, Rhode Island. Still others left New England in the late eighteenth century. Otis Williams, the great-great-grandson of Thomas I, set up shop in Buffalo, New York; Joseph Danforth, Jr., and Henry J. Danforth went to Richmond, Virginia; Thomas Danforth III migrated to Philadelphia, and apprentices trained in the Norwich shop established themselves in Baltimore, Maryland; Augusta, Georgia; and Fayetteville, North Carolina.

Of all the Danforth-trained pewterers, the most important are the Boardmans, whose mother, Sarah Danforth, was a granddaughter of the original Thomas. She married Oliver Boardman of Hartford, and their son, Thomas Danforth Boardman, born in 1784, was the first of a family of pewterers who developed "as many craftsmen in one generation as the Danforths had in four." Thomas Boardman and his brother Sherman opened a shop in Hartford, Connecticut, about 1840, from which they shipped pewterware to relatives who acted as their agents in Philadelphia and New York City. The shop's specialty was ecclesiastical pewter—Communion services designed for country churches which could not afford silver vessels.

The Boardmans span the last years of the "Eight-Inch-Plate" era and the beginning of the so-called "Coffee-Pot Period" (1825-1850), when pewterers unsuccessfully imitated the wares of silversmiths. During this

Pewter teapot, probably Britanniaware. Typical teapot form, 1845-1849. Marked "J. A. Frary," Meriden, Connecticut.

transition period a few craftsmen—Roswell Gleason of Dorchester, Massachusetts, and Israel and Oliver Trask of Beverly, in the same state, to name the most outstanding—created coffee and teapots, baptismal and sugar bowls, covered water pitchers, syrup jugs, and picture frames that were a credit to their craft. But most pewterers who worked during these years abandoned craftsmanship for factory methods in hopes of competing with wares made of glass which were coming into general use.

By 1840, most small pewtering shops had vanished. In their place, factories such as the one operated by Babbitt, Crossman and Company—this firm eventually became Reed and Barton, the famous silverware concern—began making a wide variety of articles from britannia, a "first cousin" of pewter. Because britannia contained no lead, being composed of tin, copper, and antimony, it was brighter than ordinary pewter and closely resembled silver. Moreover, it could be easily soldered and molded. Fashioned into expensive objects, britannia won instant public acceptance. As a result, Ashbil Griswold, who had opened a pewtering shop in Meriden, Connecticut, in 1808, shifted to the manufacture of britannia wares in 1830 and within a few months was employing scores of workmen. His factory, which later merged with that operated by the Rogers brothers, became the International Silver Company.

Britannia was not a fancy ware. Designed to sell cheaply, it also appealed to housewives because it was easier to shine than pewter. As the demand for both unplated and silverplated britannia increased, improved methods were developed for spinning the metal on a lathe or stamping it into shape with dies. Meanwhile, manufacturers began placing elaborate ornamentation on their plated wares in imitation of the decorations used by silversmiths.

But the public lost interest in britannia when manufacturers began offering inexpensive silverplated wares. By the end of the War Between the States, pewter had disappeared from American homes—much of it melted down for bullets—and britannia was no longer fashionable. As a result, the pewterer vanished as a craftsman and most britannia manufacturers shifted to the making of electroplated table and hollow wares.

8

Workers in Base Metals

———————————⟫⟪———————————

Although the craftsmen who worked brass, copper, iron, and tin were important artisans in America before the establishment of factories, actually little is known of them as individuals. Because they rarely stamped their products with their names or a characteristic symbol, it is extremely difficult to identify the work of any particular craftsman. Moreover, the arts of fashioning brass, copper, and tin, having much in common, were often combined. As a result, it is nearly impossible to classify those who engaged in them in specific categories.

The blacksmith was probably the first worker in base metals to ply his craft in the colonies. However, for convenience, this group has been presented alphabetically.

BRAZIERS

Little brass was made in America until the mid-eighteenth century. Therefore, American artisans worked brass the least of all the common metals. Moreover, by 1827, when the commercial mining of zinc began here—assuring an ample supply of brass—most handworkers had been replaced by factories.

Because of the scarcity of sheet brass in the colonies, most early braziers fashioned few new articles. However, they did melt down old brass and cast it in new forms. In order to conserve metal, the craftsmen of the colonial and Federal periods used a special technique known as "split brass" when fashioning round objects. They cast them in halves, each one a hollow shell, then joined the halves by brazing—soldering with brass.

Braziers had to be skilled woodworkers because, before casting an article, they had to make a wood pattern. After the pattern was shaped, it was placed in a container and completely surrounded by sand. The pattern was then removed and the cavity filled with molten brass, which was then cooled, removed from the sand, cleaned, and polished.

Besides making patterns and molds for their own use, braziers also sup-

Pair of early brass whale oil lamps.

Brass andirons with oval finials and wrought iron shafts. Late 18th century, they are stamped "J. Davis, Boston."

plied pewterers with the molds they used to fashion spoons, plates, and other objects. Spoon and plate molds had two sections and when the metal in them solidified, the mold was opened and the casting remover—the mold having first been coated with the smoke from a candle to prevent the pewter from sticking to it. Several molds were needed for such irregularly shaped objects as teapots; then the various sections were soldered together.

Most of the brass used in colonial days was scrap collected by peddlers who drove wagons about the countryside buying battered household utensils originally made in Europe. When melted down, the old brass was cast into a wide variety of articles. After listing his wares in the Maryland *Gazette* for December 6, 1759, Philip Syng, "Brass Founder from Philadelphia, Living near the Town Gate in Annapolis" informed the public that he gave "the best prices for old Brass and Copper."

Syng, like other braziers, made fireplace equipment, either fashioning it completely from brass or from iron topped with brass knobs. After the Revolution, many braziers in Boston and Philadelphia celebrated the defeat of the British by placing an eagle and thirteen stars on the tops of fireplace tools.

About the time Syng was advertising his wares, John Robertson of South Carolina and Daniel Jackson of Providence, Rhode Island, were offering stock furniture fittings, although many cabinetmakers preferred to buy their brasses from England. When the Revolution ended British trade restrictions and more brass became available, such firms as Bolt and Grew of Boston solicited customers by advertising "orders for Coach and Cabinet Furniture executed to any pattern." This company had competition from a business associate of Paul Revere, Paul Hunneman, who operated a brass foundry in Boston from the 1790's to about 1850.

Many braziers cast bells. The most famous are Pass and Stow of Philadelphia. When the bell cast in England for the Pennsylvania State House cracked upon arriving in Philadelphia in 1752, Pass and Stow were commissioned to melt down the original bell and recast another from the metal. Their first casting produced another defective bell, but their second attempt was successful. No words were ever more prophetic than the ones these craftsmen chose from Leviticus to inscribe upon this bell: "Proclaim Liberty throughout the land unto all inhabitants thereof." On July 4, 1776, Andrew Macnair, the State House bellman, tolled Pass and Stow's thrice-cast bell to announce that the Continental Congress had passed the Declaration of Independence by a unanimous vote. Ever since, the booming tones of the Liberty Bell have echoed in the hearts of all freedom-loving men.

Other Philadelphia brass founders beside Pass and Stow made bells. Daniel King specialized in horse bells which were fastened in sets on the collars of the six-horse teams which pulled Conestoga wagons loaded with

LEFT: *Combining the crafts of the wheelwright, smith, woodworker and needle-woman, the Conestoga wagon was used to carry goods to the West and produce to seacoast markets.* RIGHT: *After Revere got his "furnass agoing" in 1788, he advertised his copper and brass wares in Boston newspapers.*

merchandise from seaport towns to the interior or carried farmers' produce to the cities.

The Conestoga wagon—first built by John Carter in the Conestoga Valley of Pennsylvania—was, in itself, the work of several craftsmen, combining the skills of the wheelwright, blacksmith, weaver, and needleworker. This high, heavy wagon (weighing between 3,000 and 3,500 pounds) was fashioned from oak and poplar by the wheelwright, who designed it so that there was a downward curve in the middle of the body. This permitted the load to settle toward the center as the vehicle bumped along unpaved roads. To take up the strain, blacksmiths fitted the wagon with braces and chains, which enabled it to carry a tremendous load. The white homespun, tentlike covering was woven and sewed by the wife of one of the craftsmen or that of the purchaser of the wagon.

Tradition demanded that any wagoner who ran into difficulty on the road and had to be assisted by another teamster was duty bound to give his team's bells to the man who had helped him. Therefore, whenever the driver of a Conestoga wagon arrived at his destination he shouted proudly, "I'm here with bells on!" This phrase is still used in a slightly different form—"I'll be there with bells on!"—to denote pleasure at being invited to a social gathering.

Many gunsmiths also worked in brass, using it for trigger guards, butt plates, and the covers of patch boxes. By covering the latter with intricate engravings, these artisans added greatly to the beauty of their hand-wrought weapons. Other braziers made clock parts, surveyors' tools, compass faces, and sundials. Still others, including the Chandlees (a large family that included craftsmen of many skills) made surgical tools, particularly lancets—instruments used in blood letting, once the medical profession's cure for most ills.

However, as America became more industrialized, small shops operated by individuals who could "turn out" anything a customer desired gave way to large factories. As a result, a brass worker no longer needed to be an expert craftsman, but merely the master of a single, specialized skill. Nevertheless, artisans using hand tools and traditional methods still produce brasswork for special purposes or create decorative pieces equal in beauty to those fashioned when the craft of the brazier was honored.

COPPERSMITHS

Strangely enough, the original settlers in the American colonies ignored the large deposits of copper scattered along the eastern seaboard. Therefore, only a small quantity of copper was produced in America during the seventeenth century. Handicapped by this lack of metal, coppersmiths could do little except repair housewares which had been imported from England.

The earliest example of American copper work that can be surely identified is a weathervane in the shape of an Indian made early in the eighteenth

TOP: *Pair of brass acorn-top andirons, late 18th century. The brass wax jack in the center has pierced framework on scrolled feet and is fitted with bird-form pincers and a winder with a wood handle.* BOTTOM: *Brass and wirework fender fashioned in New England in the late 18th century.*

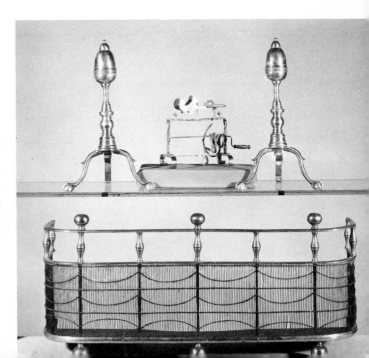

century by Shem Drowne (1683-1774) of Boston. By the time Drowne was engaged in hammering out this weathervane, copper was being extensively mined in the colonies. In 1707, the authorities of East Granby, Connecticut, had granted a company the right to work a nearby copper mine in return for a royalty of ten shillings on every ton of copper produced. It was a successful venture and, in 1737, the first colonial copper coins were minted at East Granby from ore taken from this mine.

Before the Revolution, copper was being produced in several colonies, particularly Maryland and New Jersey. Using copper from these mines, coppersmiths were able to fashion new articles. On June 29, 1738, Philadelphia's first coppersmith inserted this advertisement in the Pennsylvania *Gazette*:

Peacock Bigger, Brazier
In Market Street, near the sign of the
Indian King
Makes and sells all kinds of Copperwork

However, it is extremely doubtful that Bigger or any other eighteenth-century American coppersmith was able to supply "all kinds of Copperwork." British law forbade the erection or operation of rolling mills in the colonies; therefore, there was not enough copper for the needs of craftsmen, for copper smelted in this country had either to be sent to England

LEFT: *Robert Fulton's letter to Paul Revere ordering copper plates and rivets of "the best of copper" for his steamboat.* RIGHT: *Before houses were heated with stoves or furnaces, long-handled pans containing coals were used to warm bedsheets during the winter months.*

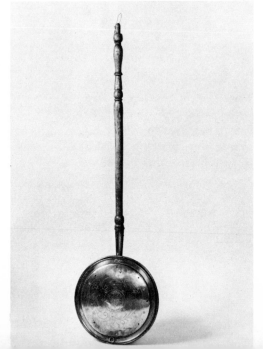

to be rolled into sheets or else hammered flat by hand—a tedious and difficult process.

It was this lack of sheet copper that forced coppersmiths to turn to other activities to make a living. After announcing in the South Carolina *Gazette and General Advertiser* for May 25, 1784, that he had moved his shop, George Ross added, "Gentlemen's lamps lighted and kept in order by the year or quarterly." About the same time, James M'Calmond, a York, Pennsylvania, coppersmith, added to his income by operating a dry goods store, while Frederick Steinman, another Pennsylvania coppersmith, opened a hardware store in Lancaster which became the oldest continuously operated establishment of its kind in the country.

No matter what else they did, all early coppersmiths made warming pans, which were used by everyone in those days of unheated houses. A warming pan can best be described as a pot attached to a long handle. Hot coals were placed in the pot—the smoke escaping through its pierced lid— and it was then used to warm cold sheets.

Charles Hanneman of Boston and a few other American coppersmiths adopted the English style of fitting a warming pan to a tapered iron handle which ended in a hook for hanging. But most warming pans made in this country had wooden handles about thirty inches long, usually made of maple but sometimes of other hardwoods.

Coppersmiths often made the bottom of the pan of copper and its lid— which fitted within the base—of brass. But no matter what the material, the lid was always decorated by having its perforations arranged to form a design, or by embossing, or engraving.

Among the other domestic articles made by coppersmiths were kettles, kitchenware, coffee and chocolate pots, pans, measures, funnels, ladles, and skimmers—all of which were advertised by Richard Collier in the Providence *Gazette* for August 6, 1763.

The ladles and skimmers made by coppersmiths were important kitchen utensils until the late nineteenth century. They were also used in the making of maple syrup and, incidentally, are still employed in candymaking. Copper ladles and skimmers were actually the products of two crafts— coppersmiths fashioned the bowls, while blacksmiths formed their ornamented, wrought-iron handles.

Collier's advertisement could have been that of most coppersmiths of his period. However, besides making household articles, coppersmiths also fabricated equipment for manufacturers of hats, soap, and cloth, as well as furnishing stills to those engaged in producing alcohol and turpentine. They also supplied bolts, braces, spikes, and other copper fittings to shipbuilders. From Paul Revere's rolling mill in Canton came 7,675 pounds of copper sheeting and 768 pounds of copper nails used to resheath the roof

ABOVE: *Revere's copper rolling mill as developed at Canton, Massachusetts.* BELOW: *Reconstruction of America's first iron works at Saugus, Massachusetts.*

of the Massachusetts State House—a covering that lasted for a century. Revere's mill also supplied the copper used in all of Robert Fulton's steamboats. It is extremely doubtful if any of these vessels would have slid down the ways if Revere had not been able to furnish the necessary copper or had been unwilling to grant Fulton the credit he so sorely needed.

Because Revere was an important figure, it is a simple task to trace his career as a coppersmith, but it is extremely difficult to compile a list of, and collect information about, the ordinary individuals who worked copper until factory-produced wares ended the era of the craftsman. For example, although twenty-six known advertisements were inserted in various papers between 1765 and 1799 by Benjamin Harbeson, who carried on the "Copperfmith's bufinefs" in Philadelphia and Lancaster during the last half of the eighteenth century, they provide few facts about him. Actually, despite laborious research by collectors of antiques, there is far less known about coppersmiths than any other American craftsmen with the exception of their fellow artisans who worked with iron or tin.

IRONWORKERS

Before the members of Sir Walter Raleigh's expedition to Roanoke Island—site of the first English settlement in North America—mysteriously vanished, they reported the discovery of iron ore. There is little doubt that Raleigh's group found bog-iron, a soft iron ore that is common in swampy regions. While the settlers of Jamestown sent a shipment of bog-iron to England in 1608, the finding of ore deposits in other colonies prompted attempts to build ironworks. Most of them failed.

The first successful iron foundry in America was established in Saugus, Massachusetts, about 1645. The works was authorized "on condition that the inhabitants of this jurisdiction shall be furnished with all sorts of barr iron for their use . . ."

Colonial blacksmiths used both local "barr iron" and the more expensive iron imported from England in their shops. They made shoes for horses and oxen, pots, kettles, latches, hinges, gates, fences, andirons, cranes, and many other objects, including tools. Every blacksmith—and colonial registers reveal that a considerable number practiced the craft—had at least one shovel block, the mold used to cast the bowl of a shovel. A well-equipped smithy also contained a large collection of other molds, known technically as templates. Early blacksmiths were also called upon to fashion special tools for customers who wanted to use them for a particular purpose. Today, when such articles appear in shops or at auctions, neither the seller nor the buyer is apt to know what they were called, and rarely has any idea how they were used.

Nor, in most cases, do we know who made them. Yet, no craftsmen were more important to their communities, and it is unfortunate that all that is known about the majority of them is their names and the location of their shops.

Occasionally, however, colonial records reveal something about these men. Because the authorities ordered William Chessbrough to abandon his forge at Wequetquok, Connecticut, and establish another in New London, "for fear he would repair guns for the Indians," we know that this early blacksmith made guns, as did a number of his fellow craftsmen who worked in the vicinity of Lancaster, Pennsylvania. They produced the "Kentucky Rifle"—so named because it was used by Daniel Boone and other frontiersmen.

But, for the most part, blacksmiths willingly fashioned anything their customers demanded, from cast iron kettles (first molded in Carver, Massachusetts, in 1730) to smoke jacks. The latter were iron fans attached to fireplace spits which rotated when the rising heat turned the fans. Early blacksmiths were also called upon to make latches and hinges of various types. Although they produced utilitarian articles, these craftsmen often ornamented them, decorating latch plates with animal, floral or geometric designs; ending the handles of spits in the form of flowers; or hammering the base of a trivet—a low, three-legged stand for hot vessels—into pleasing shapes.

By 1750, despite British regulations, black smoke was pouring from the chimneys of iron furnaces throughout the colonies. None were more prosperous than those in Pennsylvania where there was an ample supply of iron ore worked by skilled artisans who were supervised by expert ironmasters. Of all the ironware produced in Pennsylvania none are more famous than the region's cast-iron stoves.

LEFT: *Early 19th century iron steelyard or balance. Marked "J. Hammond. E. Brookfield" (Massachusetts).* RIGHT: *Sturdy in construction but having a graceful form, these hand-wrought iron latch handles were made by a blacksmith.*

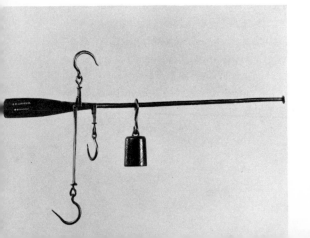

Before the invention of stoves, women had to cook at fireplaces like this one. Note the many items of iron, the pewter plate, the wooden settle, and the quilt held by the model.

Although stoves made of soapstone plates bound together with iron were used in New England at an early date, stoves were not common in colonial America. Most settlers relied on fireplaces to cook their food and warm their houses. But as fireplaces threw very little heat in comparison to the amount of wood they consumed, even countryfolk—who did not have to purchase fuel—hastened to buy a cast-iron stove molded after the one invented by Benjamin Franklin in 1747, which he never bothered to patent. Because this stove stood out from the wall, it warmed a room better than a fireplace, which allowed most of the heat to escape up the chimney.

While the Franklin stove was first made in Pennsylvania, the foundries in that colony are better known for another type of stove—a reproduction of one made in Germany and the Scandinavian countries. These stoves featured plates decorated with Biblical scenes and moral axioms. Because they could purchase a stove in America exactly like the one they used in their homeland, "Pennsylvania Dutch" immigrants did not bring stoves with them to the New World.

The original five-plate stoves had no outlet to the room in which they

LEFT: *Franklin stove: this stove is noteworthy for its ornamentation and the large apron designed to catch the ashes.* RIGHT: *In the late eighteenth century, ten-plate, cast-iron stoves with space for cooking replaced stoves with fewer plates used for heating. This one was made by Baron Stiegel at Elizabeth Furnace.*

stood. Instead, they were fitted to a hole out in the back wall of a fireplace in an adjoining room. Fuel was added from the fireplace, and, as the iron plates heated, they warmed their surroundings. Later, six- and ten-plate stoves were made and were used not only for heating but also for cooking, a fuel door being cut into their sides. The door spoiled the ornamentation, but housewives didn't mind. They found it easier to cook on a stove than over a fireplace fire.

One of the first Pennsylvania ironmasters to fabricate ten-plate stoves was "Baron" Stiegel of glassmaking fame. As general-manager of the furnace, owned by his father-in-law, Stiegel supervised the casting of many five-plate stoves. However, few of them were embellished with intricate ornamentation or religious scenes. Typically, Stiegel "put an end to this waste of good advertising space." At first he cast couplets flattering his father-in-law on the plates, but when he became sole owner of the works, the plates read:

Baron Stiegel ist der Mann   Baron Stiegel is the man
Der die ofen machen kann   Who knows how to make stoves

Besides making Franklin and European-type stoves, Stiegel also developed a pipeless stove. In addition, he manufactured machinery used in the refining of molasses and shipped it to the West Indies. Eventually, he employed nearly one hundred workmen and became one of the most successful ironmasters in the New World.

Meanwhile, the iron industry had become well established and when the Revolution began, the forges of blacksmiths and the furnaces of ironmasters were able to furnish supplies to the Continental Army. Perhaps the greatest contribution of ironworkers to the cause of freedom was the building of a chain which was strung across the Hudson River at West Point, New York, to keep the British from reaching Albany.

Peter Townsend, the ironmaster at Ward and Coulton's Furnace at Sterling, New York, was responsible for this chain. Aided by sixty blacksmiths furloughed from the Continental Army, who worked day and night, he forged the chain and the twelve tons of anchors required to hold it in place in six weeks. As each section was completed it was hauled over snow-covered roads to West Point, where the sections were joined and the chain floated across the river on a log boom to which the anchors were attached.

Benedict Arnold, then in command of the fort at West Point, after deciding to betray his country, devised a scheme for destroying the chain which he planned to turn over to the British. Fortunately, Arnold's treason was discovered and, withstanding all attempts by man or nature to sever its tremendous links, the chain remained in place until the end of the Revolution.

With the coming of peace, factory-made ironware began to take the place of hand-wrought articles. However, blacksmiths still continued to pump their bellows in city shops, being called upon to do repair work and to shoe horses. Meanwhile, along the western frontier, the ancient craft of the smith was furnishing household utensils and tools, while in New Orleans, Louisiana, and Charleston, South Carolina, Negro slaves, trained as blacksmiths, were creating America's most famous wrought ironwork. Hammering their iron at white heat, these craftsmen adapted the intricate

Connecting pin and link of the "Great Chain" hand-forged by colonial blacksmiths that was stretched across the Hudson at West Point, New York, to prevent the British from reaching Albany by boat.

patterns of French and Spanish ironwork to form grills, fences, and railings of exceptional beauty.

Today, Longfellow's mighty smith who swung his heavy sledge "with measured beat and slow" no longer exists. Not only has the welder's arc taken the place of forge, hammer, and anvil, but also machine shops and factories—often employing metals other than iron—fabricate most of the articles once made by blacksmiths. Horseshoeing, for many years the major occupation of the craft, is now an almost vanished skill, practiced by but a few specialists.

However, the ancient traditions of the blacksmithing craft have not been completely forgotten. A few individuals in studio-shops still continue to work white hot iron with hand tools. Their wares, like the wrought iron of yesteryear, combine the skill of the craftsman with the creative ability of the artist.

TINSMITHS

No one knows when man first fabricated tin plate (which is not a dish but a thin sheet of iron coated with melted tin). However, by 1620, the year the Pilgrims landed at Plymouth, tin-plating was a well-established industry in Germany. Fifty years later, tin plate was being produced in tremendous amounts in England, but to prevent possible competition with British manufactories, none was shipped to the North American colonies. Nor could tinsmiths of the New World hammer iron bars into sheets and then dip them in a "tin pot"—there was plenty of iron in the colonies but no known supply of tin until its discovery in Goshen, Connecticut, in 1829.

But long before this vein of tin was unearthed, Connecticut was producing tinware. About 1740, Edward and William Patterson, two Irish-trained tinsmiths, opened a shop in the town of Berlin. The Patterson brothers must have had powerful friends in England, for they were allowed to import tin plate. With it they made household articles and, like all members of their craft, fashioned them by hand.

Early tinsmiths first outlined the pattern for the various sections of an article on a large sheet of tin, then cut them out with huge shears. After shaping the parts into their required form with tools, the artisans turned the edges of adjoining pieces by beating them on an anvil—which strengthened the seams—and then soldered the pieces together, re-enforcing the edges with iron wire. Eventually, machines—invented by Seth Peck—which were driven by water power were used to turn the edges. This reduced the time it took to fashion tinware and, as a result, lowered its cost.

Originally, the Pattersons sold their products only in Berlin and nearby towns. Once the local market was satisfied, the Pattersons packed tinware

ABOVE: *Strangely enough, some of the famous ironwork in the French Quarter of New Orleans was made in Pennsylvania, but much of it was fashioned by slaves trained as blacksmiths.* BELOW: *Interior of a blacksmith shop in Byfield, Massachusetts, operated by the same family for over two hundred years.*

Early tinware. Candle mold, canister, tole tray, pierced-tin foot warmer, and sconce.

Tin locomotive weathervane from the cupola of the West Medford, Massachusetts, railroad station.

into baskets and traveled up and down Connecticut on horseback, seeking customers. They found them in great numbers, and this led them to hire salesmen. Tin peddlers, their wagons loaded with Patterson-made tinware, jolted over the rough roads from Berlin to the plantations of the South and the frontier settlements of the West.

Meanwhile, Patterson-trained apprentices were opening their own shops in Berlin and in other parts of the country. There was also competition from tinsmiths who had learned the craft elsewhere. For example, Benjamin Marsall advertised in the Pennsylvania *Chronicle* for April 27, 1767, that he "Still Continues to make and sell all kinds of plain, painted, japanned and planished Tinware."

Marsall was not the first to sell decorated tinware in this country, for as early as 1711, Nehemiah Partridge of Boston was painting imported japanned tin plate. Other tinsmiths must have engaged in the same activity, but there is little evidence of their output. Not only was most early tinware unmarked but also much of it has long been discarded, due to the rusting of the iron beneath the plating of tin.

After the Revolution, tin plate was no longer in short supply and the number of tinsmiths increased. During the last decade of the eighteenth century, members of the craft were advertising in nearly all large cities. Perhaps the most interesting of these advertisements is that of Thomas Passmore, who worked in Philadelphia between 1794 and 1800. It lists all the articles made by Passmore in alphabetical order including "Argyles for gravy" and "Speaking trumpets."

In 1798, Zachariah Brackett Stevens opened a tin shop in Stevens Point, now Westbrook, Maine. He may have had a business arrangement with Paul Revere, for Revere's nephew, Phillip Rose, went to Stevens Point to work as a tinsmith. Stevens' sons, Samuel and Alfred, took over their father's business in 1830, but the quality of their work was greatly inferior to his and the shop closed down in 1842. During their operation of the works, the Stevens brothers had competition from nearly a dozen other tinsmiths in the same section of Maine with combined sales totaling nearly thirty thousand dollars.

However, the major portion of tinware made in America during the first four decades of the nineteenth century was fashioned by Connecticut craftsmen. The list of their products is a long one: cooking utensils, churns, milk pans and pails, fancy wares, ovens, measures, weathervanes, deedboxes, candlesticks and molds, and various lighting devices. The latter included Betty lamps, branched chandeliers, candle stands, and lanterns of all types.

It would be interesting to know if a tinsmith or a wood carver made the doughnut cutter used in 1763, when America's first doughnut shop was opened in New York City. However, we do know that tinsmiths fashioned rolling pins to which pastry dough would not stick, made brown-bread tins, cookie cutters, and pie crimpers. One of the many articles made by tin-smiths for use in the kitchen was the pie closet. It consisted of a wooden frame to which sheets of pierced tin were tacked from the inside, the door being paneled in the same way. The holes allowed air to circulate over the pies, but were small enough to keep out ants and flies.

Besides being used for pie closets and foot warmers—which held a small lamp, candle, or hot coals—and other practical articles, pierced tin was also employed for its decorative effect. Perhaps the most attractive of all early tin trays are those known as "lace-edge trays." Their edges were pierced with diamond, oval, square, and wedge shaped tools—a technique devised by that master metalworker, Paul Revere.

In addition to painting and piercing tinware, craftsmen also decorated it with punched work—raised or embossed designs. This was done by hammering a blunt tool against the tin on the reverse of the side which would show the decoration. Some tinsmiths also engraved their handiwork with a sharp instrument. But the most popular decorated tinware was "toleware" —household articles made of painted tin.

Only japanned tin could be ornamented with painted geometric designs, flowers, scenes, animals, or human figures. The japanning of tin originated in the Orient—probably inspired by the Chinese craft of lacquering or varnishing wood—and Europeans soon mastered the process. Great quantities of japanned tin were made at Pontypool, England, where an excellent varnish capable of withstanding extreme heat and which coated tin with a smooth, hard surface was developed. Huge amounts of this tin were shipped to

LEFT: *Early 19th century hand-decorated tea caddy, made in Connecticut.* RIGHT: *This small tin trinket or document box was made in Connecticut in the early 19th century. It is black with red, green, yellow, and white decorations.*

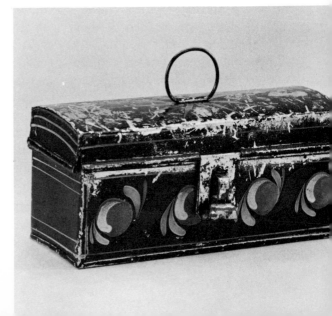

Representative early 19th century brilliantly hand-decorated toleware. From left: document box, mug, coffee pot, sugar bowl, and canister.

America during the latter part of the eighteenth century.

While much of it arrived in the form of finished and painted wares, local tinsmiths also imported sheets of japanned tin and fashioned it into trays, tea caddies, and other articles. Before these were sold they were painted with bright decorations against a field of solid color. The most popular background color was black, but blue, Chinese red, green, white, and yellow were also used, as was a background which imitated tortoise shell. Frequently, trained artists were hired to do the painting of the designs, but it was commonly done by the tinsmiths themselves. They either ornamented their wares freehand or applied the designs by means of a stencil, using the same technique employed to decorate a Hitchcock chair.

As the nineteenth century ended, the demand for tinware lessened. Today, the craft is kept alive in many American schools which feature vocational training. However, such honest artisans as William Manning who expressed the wish that ". . . an assiduous Attention will insure him protection of a discerning Public" in his advertisement inserted in the *Gazette of the United States* on May 25, 1799, would not be pleased—for those who are being taught to master shears, hammer, and soldering iron no longer bear the proud title of tinsmith, but are known instead as sheet-metal workers.

9

Patch, Paste, and Pen Crafts

In 1716, the Boston *News Letter*, the first newspaper published in what was to be called the United States of America, carried this advertisement:

This is to give Notice, that at the house of Mr. George Brownwell, late School Master in Hanover Street Boston, are all sorts of Millernary Works done . . . and also young Gentlewomen and Children taught all sorts of fine Works as Quilting, Feather-Work . . . Embroidering in a new way, Turkey-Work for Hankerchiefs . . . flourishing and plain Work, and Dancing cheaper than ever was taught in Boston, Brocaded Work for Hankerchiefs and short Aprons upon Muslin, artificial Flowers work'd with a Needle.

Many other advertisements for embroidery and needlework schools can be found in copies of pre-Revolutionary American newspapers. However, long before such schools were established, colonial women were experts in the craft of needlework. Those who lived in rural districts had to spin, weave, and dye cloth, as well as sew it. Meanwhile, city dwellers who could afford to employ "taylors" worked embroidery, for it was not considered proper for a woman to "sit in idleness." But whether rich or poor, resident of a thriving seaport town or of a crude settlement, all women of the colonial period made patchwork quilts.

Patchwork is a craft that has been practiced "ever since the first woven cloth wore out in spots," but in no other country has the making of patchwork quilts become so highly developed a craft as in America. Even today, when machinery has made inexpensive patchwork quilts available to all, home craftsmen still duplicate the handiwork of countless unknown women.

There are two kinds of patchwork quilts, pieced and appliquéd. In the first, the patches are sewn together by means of a seam and, in the second, small patches of cloth are laid on larger pieces and then hemmed. While piecework is a characteristic of American quilt-making, appliquéd quilts are common, as are many quilts which combine both methods. Originally, the patches were fitted together in haphazard fashion, making "crazy" or "hit-and-miss" patterns, but gradually distinct designs evolved. Most of them are geometric: Roman Square, Philadelphia Pavement, Star of Bethlehem, and Log Cabin, among many others. While the majority of patterns were known from Plymouth to Georgia, their names often varied from place to place.

Quilting not only provided warm coverings for beds in poorly heated homes but also filled a social need. While their husbands exhibited animals and crops at local fairs, the women displayed their quilts. Then, too, neighbors could be invited to a "quilting bee," and such affairs were gala events. They usually ended with supper and dancing—the men arriving when the quilting was finished. Quilting bees must also have been looked forward to by romantic young people, for in one of his most famous ballads, Stephen Foster, the well-known American composer wrote:

> *In the sky the bright stars glittered,*
> *On the banks the pale moon shone,*
> *And 'twas from Aunt Dinah's quilting party*
> *I was seeing Nellie home.*

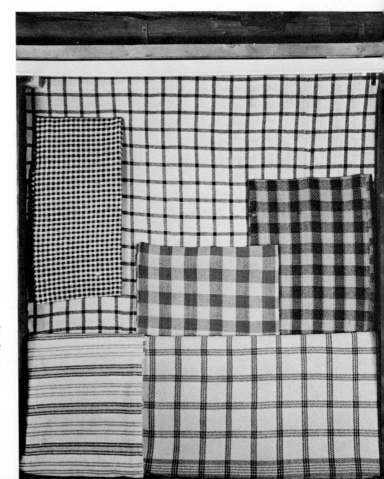

A display of New England homespun linsey-woolsey, a fabric of many uses in early America.

A cotton patchwork quilt, Sunburst pattern.

Handmade quilts are still sewn in America today, like this one by the author's mother in the Log Cabin pattern.

CREWEL-WORK
AND
NEEDLEPOINT

Crewel-work—em-
broidering with yarn—
was a colorful means
of textile decoration.
Throughout the colo-
nial period it was ap-
plied to bed hangings,
coverlets, upholstering,
and clothing.

Needlepoint was an-
other popular form of
embroidery, which add-
ed gay color to the
household.

Petit point *and crewel work of the mid-eighteenth century.*

Few pre-Revolutionary quilts have survived their innumerable washings, and most early specimens displayed in museums date from the 1830's. However, later examples of the quilt-maker's craft are very common. In some cases, a quilt's pattern simplifies the task of determining when it was made. For example, the Little Giant pattern honors Stephen A. Douglas, who debated with Lincoln, and Fifty-Four-Forty commemorates this country's dispute with England over the boundary of the Oregon territory. But whether faded or bright, designed to celebrate a current event or fashioned in a traditional pattern, the patchwork quilts of yesteryear offer proof that the women who made them had the true craftsman's appreciation of form and were masters with a needle.

The warmth of a quilt-covered bed was soon forgotten, however, when one stepped out onto the cold floor of these early homes. While the wealthy could import floor coverings from Europe or stay abed until a servant fed new fuel to the glowing ashes in a fireplace, poor people could not afford such luxuries. Therefore, at a very early date, American women began making braided and hooked rugs. At first they fashioned the latter by pulling strips of colored cloth through a base of coarse linen, creating their own designs. Then, shortly after the War Between the States, Edward Sands Frost started a rug-pattern manufactory in Biddeford, Maine. His full-size designs were applied to a piece of burlap on which the hooking was done. After 1870, Frost stenciled his patterns in full color, but his wares were soon imitated by competitors, including a firm in Dayton, Ohio, which also advertised a mechanical hooker—a device true home crafters refused to use then, and do not use now.

The availability of machine-made, woven, stamped, and printed textiles did not bring an end to needlecraft. In many cases women could not afford to buy "store goods" and, even if they could, sewing and embroidery were considered "proper relaxation for females"—actually, in many cases, the only relaxation women enjoyed. As a result, not only did needlewomen make necessary articles, but they also covered everything from plant pots to fire screens with *petit point* and crewel. A few women supported themselves by sewing, either working in private homes or in unholstering shops. One actually established a specialized textile manufacturing plant in 1834. This pioneer woman industrialist was Sally McFadden, who opened America's first commercial flag factory in New York City.

Today, many women do *petit point* or crewel and use their handiwork to cover handbags and the backs and seats of chairs. However, no longer does a novice with a needle learn various stitches by making a sampler—a piece of cloth on which either the alphabet, numerals, bits of verse, family history, various designs, scenes, or the Lord's Prayer are worked. Because they were usually sewn by young girls, samplers often show a lack of skill, but one can understand the pride of five-year-old Mary Smith who placed two alphabets on her sampler—one in capital, the other in small letters—and then stitched: "Mary Smith is my name and with my nedel I wrought the same."

Although women specialized in home crafts that would produce useful articles, they also designed them to brighten their surroundings. However, it wasn't until the mid-nineteenth century when home furnishings became very elaborate that women engaged in "art" crafts that would enable them to "decorate" their already over-crowded parlors. It became fashionable for women to attend art classes and to learn how to paint flowers on china, and every "female seminary" gave instruction in watercoloring.

Even if a woman could not afford to study china painting or had no talent as a watercolorist, she still could engage in a craft. Anyone could do potichomania—paste bits of colored paper flat against the inner wall of glass vessels, then fill them with plaster. Potichomania jars "for making imitation china vases" were advertised in Philadelphia in 1857, and potichomania balls were also available. They were made of glass, were quite

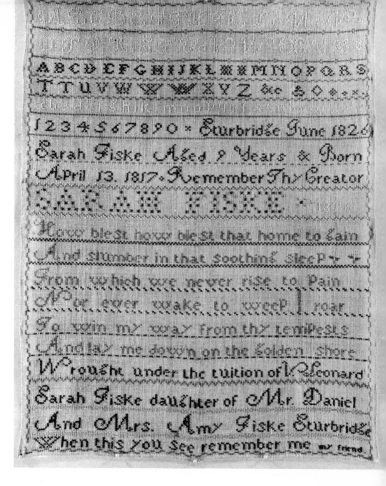

Painstakingly embroidered with the alphabet, numbers, her name, the date, and a verse, this sampler shows that nine-year-old Sarah Fiske was a clever needlewoman.

large, and the paper was applied through a small opening.

While husbands used jig saws to fashion the scrolls and frets so admired by Victorian housekeepers—who evidently didn't mind spending hours dusting—wives engaged in pyrography. This consisted of burning designs, pictures, or vessels on a piece of soft wood with a red hot tool. Some women became quite expert in this craft and used a poker to "paint" both landscapes and portraits, which are now known as "hot-poker pictures" to collectors.

The majority of women who engaged in home crafts never thought of selling their handiwork. However, a few such as those on Martha's Vineyard, an island off the Massachusetts' coast, wove blankets and knitted gloves and socks to support themselves while their husbands were chasing whales in the Pacific on vessels that might not return to their home port for two or three years. The women of Franklin County, New Jersey, also helped support their families by a unique craft until the 1840's. After their husbands collected and bored holes in shells, the wives strung them, and the necklaces were sold to traders who needed wampum for barter with the Indians.

This Courting Letter was brought to Pennsylvania, probably from Alsace, in 1812 and is one of the finest known. It greatly influenced the art of fraktur in America.

Perhaps the most unusual craft practiced by women in the period between the early eighteenth century and the 1880's was hairwork. It consisted of weaving human hair into flowers, fruit, portraits, foliage, or rings. The finished product was often presented to an admirer as a love token!

Before printed books replaced written ones, dedicated monks had toiled —sometimes for years—to fashion a book by hand. With painstaking care they embellished their parchment manuscripts with flowing colors and gold, creating gloriously adorned title pages, pictures of animals and men, and initial letters astonishingly rich in invention and design. Then, as the press took the place of pen and brush, the art of illuminated writing became an almost forgotten craft.

However, most early printed books resembled the handwritten ones made by the monks—although they lacked illumination—because the first men to practice the printer's craft attempted to reproduce in type the lettering done in monasteries. Among the type faces they used was "fraktur" which consisted of Gothic letters "broken" into long sweeping lines and decorative flourishes.

Actually, there was nothing new about fraktur. Adapted from the hand illumination of the monks, *fraktur-schrifen*—literally "writing in Gothic type"—had been a skill of experienced penmen ever since the eleventh century. When the people we now call the Pennsylvania Dutch fled religious persecution in Alsace, Bavaria, Germany, Holland, and Switzerland and sought a new life in Penn's Woods, they brought with them the craft of fraktur. In time, using goose-quill pens, cat's hair brushes, and bright red, golden yellow, soft blue, and misty green paints compounded from traditional formulas, they developed a folk art which featured painted decoration and elegant writing.

Originally, Pennsylvania fraktur, like that of the Old World, was used solely for religious purposes. The earliest examples were executed at the Ephrata Cloister in Lancaster County where Conrad Beissel founded a religious community in 1728. In the "Writing Room" at Ephrata, using the techniques of medieval monks, the women of the colony copied and illuminated devotional song books and other manuscripts. Eventually, Beissel's followers acquired a printing press, but they still continued to use hand illumination to decorate their publications. The most famous book issued at Ephrata was *The Martyr's Mirror*. It appeared in 1748 and was the work of fifteen men who spent three years translating, printing, decorating, and binding fifteen hundred copies in leather tanned by other members of the group.

By the late eighteenth century, fraktur was no longer used only to embellish religious books but also was being employed on birth, baptism, confirmation, and marriage certificates. At first, clergymen and schoolmasters made these documents, but during the nineteenth century most of them were fashioned by itinerant artists who wandered about with their samples of handwriting, decorative designs, pens, brushes, and paints.

Fraktur illumination and Gothic lettering were taught in the German community schools of Pennsylvania until the establishment of a state-wide English school system about 1850. A schoolmaster was not only expected to "act as janitor, singing teacher and moral guardian for his young pupils," but also was required to be an expert penman. Fraktur was taught by having pupils copy a *Vorschrift* which consisted of a verse of the Bible, with letters of the alphabet below, as well as the numbers from one to ten. ABC books also featured fraktur, each letter of the alphabet introducing a Bible verse or a moral precept. As a reward for good work, pupils received a handwritten motto or religious verse surrounded by a decorative design.

In 1819, Johann Krauss of Allentown made the schoolmaster's task easier by publishing a book which not only explained the proper method of writing Gothic letters but also gave instructions for making, mixing, and fixing colors. Krauss' manual was followed by many others, but as each

THE PHILOSOPHER AND SHEPHERD.

1791.

This example of Pennsylvania fraktur, in brush and pen design, is dated 1791. The hand-painted work is done in soft browns, tan, green, and dull red; the writing is brown.

piece of fraktur work was individually designed, no two pieces are ever exactly alike, whether created by schoolboys or professionals.

Among the latter were Francis Portzeline of Union City, Daniel Schumaker of Schuykill County, and August Bauman, a veteran of the War Between the States, who worked at his craft until the beginning of the twentieth century. Bauman used modern sales methods—upon arriving in a town he first went to the pastor and inquired who had been born, baptized, or married since his last visit, then he called on his prospective customers. Another important fraktur worker was Heinrich Otto, who also decorated dower chests—the Pennsylvania equivalent of the modern hope chest.

These men and the many unknown craftsmen who lettered and decorated bookplates, ornamental pieces to hang on the wall, deeds, family registers, "house blessings," legal documents, primers for school children, New Year greetings, and valentines combined traditional German folk art designs with motifs derived from their New World surroundings. As a result, along with hearts, geometric forms, and complicated designs, they surrounded their lettering with strange-looking birds as well as doves, parrots, peacocks, and eagles. Other motifs include such mythological subjects as mermaids and unicorns, Biblical scenes and flowers. No flower was used more than the tulip, because in German it was commonly accepted as a variation of the Holy Lily—its three petals symbolizing the Trinity.

While fraktur artists paid little attention to perspective when reproducing human figures or scenes, they always showed great imagination—one created a birth certificate which pictures a clock showing the exact time the child was born! Early fraktur features soft colors, and the lettering is

In attics, barns, and shops are many articles from America's earlier days, all too few of them unfortunately, handmade, but all of them treasured as a link with the past.

obviously more important than the decoration; later fraktur stresses the ornamentation which is done in bold, bright hues, and the lettering is not so carefully done. Moreover, as the years passed, except for the work of elderly professionals, the printing and the handwriting were done in Roman, rather than Gothic letters. However, fraktur ornamentation became so lively and colorful that it served as an inspiration for craftsmen who fashioned pottery, wove cloth, blew glassware, wrought iron into gates, or painted furniture. Adapting the motifs of fraktur to their own use, these artisans evolved the style of decoration known today as "Pennsylvania Dutch."

In 1876, the first public display of antiques in America was held as part of the Centennial Exposition in Philadelphia. After viewing this exhibit, many visitors, upon returning home, prowled through their attics and barns, hoping to find a valuable piece of china, glass, or furniture among the dust-covered accumulations of discarded articles stored under eaves and in unused lofts. Few found treasures, but out of this search came a widespread interest in objects made by American craftsmen before the Industrial Revolution.

As indicated, most American handmade useful and ornamental articles have vanished. Fortunately, those that have survived are generally of the highest quality and workmanship. Cherished as heirlooms, collected by both individuals and museums, not only do these links with the past show how people once lived, but they also have such beauty of style and ornamentation that they are reproduced by manufacturers of modern household furnishings.

No one book can describe fully the lives and the creations of all those who worked with clay, glass, metals, and wood in America before the establishment of factories. However, those who have appeared briefly on these pages are typical of the American craftsman, whose handiwork shows that he who works with his hands is a laborer; he who works with his head and hands is a mechanic; but he who works with his head, hands, and heart is an artist.

Selected Bibliography

The bibliography that follows is but a partial list of sources consulted. In compiling it the author has, for the most part, included only titles designed to give a general picture of the origin and growth of American handicrafts. Therefore, the attention of the reader who desires specific information about a particular craftsman or regional craftsmanship is directed to the *Reader's Guide to Periodical Literature* which indexes articles that have appeared in such publications as *Antiques, Hobbies,* and *Magazine of Art.* Not only is the author indebted to the specialists who wrote these articles, but also to those responsible for various museum bulletins, newspaper articles, and privately printed monographs.

BACKGROUND READING

Dow, George F. *The Arts and Crafts in New England, 1704-1775.* Topsfield, Massachusetts: The Wayside Press, 1927.

Dreppard, Carl W. *Dictionary of American Antiques.* New York: Doubleday & Company, 1952.

———. *Pioneer America.* New York: Doubleday & Company, 1949.

———. *The Primer of American Antiques.* New York: Doubleday & Company, 1944.

Dyer, Walter A. *Early American Craftsmen.* New York: The Century Company, 1915.

Eberlien, Harold D. *The Practical Book of American Antiques.* Philadelphia:

J. B. Lippincott Company, 1927.

———. *Early American Arts and Crafts.* Philadelphia: J. B. Lippincott Company, 1916.

Guild, Lurell, *The Geography of American Antiques.* New York: Doubleday, Page & Company, 1927.

Ramsey, F. G. G. (ed) *The Concise Encyclopedia of Antiques.* New York: Hawthorne Books, 1955.

Rawson, Marion. *Candle Days: The Story of Early American Arts and Implements.* New York: The Century Company, 1927.

Train, Arthur K. *The Story of Everyday Things.* New York: Harper & Brothers, 1941.

BASE METALS

Burgess, Frederick W. *Chats on Old Copper and Brass*. New York: F. A. Stokes Company, 1914.

Freeman, Larry. *Light on Old Lamps*. Watkins Glen, New York: Century House, 1955.

Gould, Mr. and Mrs. Glen G. *Period Lighting Fixtures*. New York: Dodd, Mead & Company, 1928.

Gould, Mary E. *Antique Tin and Toleware: Its History and Romance*. Rutland, Vermont: C. E. Tuttle Company, 1958.

Hayward, Arthur H. *Colonial Lighting*. Boston: B. J. Brimmer Company, 1923.

Moore, N. *Old Pewter, Brass, Copper and Sheffield Plate*. New York: F. A. Stokes Company, 1905.

Pierce, Josephine H. *Fire on the Hearth*. Springfield, Massachusetts: The Pond-Ekberg Company, 1951.

Rawson, Marion M. *Handwrought Ancestors*. New York: E. P. Dutton and Company, 1936.

CHINA AND PORCELAIN

Barber, Edwin A. *Catalogue of American Potteries and Porcelains*. Philadelphia: Pennsylvania Museum, 1893.

———. *Lead Glazed Pottery*. Philadelphia: Pennsylvania Museum, 1907.

———. *Marks of American Potters*. Philadelphia: Patterson & White Company, 1904.

———. *The Pottery and Porcelain of the United States*. New York: G. P. Putnam's Sons, 1901.

Barret, Richard C. *Bennington Pottery and Porcelain*. New York: Crown Publishers, 1958.

Jervis, W. P. *The Encyclopedia of Ceramics*. New York: Blanchard, 1902.

Pitkin, Albert H. *Early American Folk Pottery*. Hartford: 1918.

Prime, William C. *Pottery and Porcelain of All Times and Nations*. New York: Harper, 1878.

Ramsay, John. *American Potters and Pottery*. Boston: Hale, Cushman & Flint, 1939.

Spargo, John. *Early American Pottery and China*. Garden City, New York: Garden City Publishing Company, 1948.

———. *The Potters and Potteries of Bennington*. Boston: Houghton Mifflin Company, 1926.

Watkins, Lura W. *Early New England Potters and Their Wares*. Cambridge, Massachusetts: Harvard University Press, 1950.

CLOCKS

Chamberlain, Paul M. *It's About Time*. New York: Richard Smith, 1941.

Dreppard, Carl W. *American Clocks and Clockmakers*. Garden City, New York: Doubleday & Company, 1947.

Hering, D. W. *The Lure of the Clock*. New York: New York University Press, 1932.

Jerome, Chauncey. *History of the American Clock Business for the Past Sixty Years and the Life of Chauncey Jerome*. New Haven, Connecticut: F. C. Dayton, Jr., 1860.

Nutting, Wallace. *The Old Clock Book*. Garden City, New York, 1935.

Palmer, Brooks. *The Book of American Clocks*. New York: Macmillan, 1950.

FURNITURE

Bjerkoe, Ethel H. *The Cabinetmakers of America*. New York: Doubleday & Company, 1957.

Cornelius, Charles O. *Furniture Masterpieces of Duncan Phyfe*. New York: Doubleday, Page & Company, 1922.

Cousins, Frank, and Riley, Philip M. *The Woodcarver of Salem—Samuel McIntire*. Boston: Little, Brown and Company, 1919.

Dreppard, Carl W. *Handbook of Antique Chairs*. New York: Doubleday & Company, 1948.

Eberlein, H. D. and McClure, Abbot. *The Practical Book of Period Furniture*. Philadelphia: J. B. Lippincott Company, 1914.

Holloway, Edward S. *American Furniture and Decoration, Colonial and Federal*. Philadelphia: J. B. Lippincott Company, 1928.

Kettell, Russell H. *The Pine Furniture of New England*. New York: Doubleday & Company, 1929.

Lyon, Irving W. *The Colonial Furniture of New England*. Boston: Houghton Mifflin Company, 1925.

Miller, Edgar G., Jr. *The Standard Book of American Furniture*. New York: Greystone Press, 1950.

Nutting, Wallace. *Furniture Treasury*. (3 vols.) Framingham, Massachusetts: Old America Company, 1928.

GLASS

Belknap, E. M. *Milk Glass*. New York: Crown Publishers, 1949.

Bergstrom, E. H. *Old Glass Paperweights*. Chicago: The Lakeside Press, 1940.

Diamond, Freda. *The Story of Glass*. New York: Harcourt, Brace and Company, 1953.

Dreppard, Carl W. *The ABC'S of Old Glass*. New York: Doubleday & Company, 1949.

Knittle, R. M. *Early American Glass*. New York: The Century Company, 1937.

Lee, Ruth Webb. *Early American Pressed Glass*. Northborough, Mass.: 1931.

———. *Sandwich Glass*. Northborough, Mass.: 1939.

———. *Victorian Glass*. Northborough, Mass.: 1944.

———. *Nineteenth-Century Art Glass*. New York: M. Barrows & Company,

1952.

——— and Rose, J. H. *American Glass Cup Plates*. Northborough, Mass.: 1948.

McClinton, Katherine M. *American Glass*. New York: The World Publishing Company, 1950.

McKearin, G. S. and Helen. *American Glass*. New York: Crown Publishers, 1941.

———. *Two Hundred Years of American Blown Glass*. New York: Doubleday & Company, 1950.

Schrijver, Elka, *Glass and Crystal*. (2 vols.) New York: Universe Books, 1965.

Van Rensselaer, S. *Early American Bottles and Flasks*. Peterborough, N. H. No date.

Watkins, Lura W. *Cambridge Glass*. Boston: Little, Brown, 1930.

NEEDLECRAFT

Bolton, Ethel S. and Coe, Eva J. *American Samplers*. Boston: Massachusetts Society of the Colonial Dames of America, 1921.

Finley, Ruth. *Old Patchwork Quilts and the Women Who Made Them*. Philadelphia: J. B. Lippincott Company, 1929.

Hall, Eliza C. *A Book of Hand-Woven Coverlets*. Boston: Little, Brown, 1914.

Waugh, Elizabeth, and Foley, Edith. *Collecting Hooked Rugs*. New York: The Century Company, 1927.

Webster, Marie D. *Quilts, Their Story and How to Make Them*. New York: Tudor Publishing Company, 1943.

PENNSYLVANIA FOLK ART

Adams, Ruth. *Pennsylvania Dutch Art*. New York: The World Publishing Company, 1950.

Sabine, Ellen S. *American Folk Art*. Princeton, New Jersey: D. Van Nostrand Company, 1958.

Sneed, Jane. *Pennsylvania Dutch Designs*. Media, Pennsylvania: 1955.

PEWTER

Jacobs, Carl. *Guide to American Pewter*. New York: McBride, 1957.

Kerfoot, J. B. *American Pewter*. New York: Bonzana Books, 1924.

SILVER

Avery, C. Louise. *Early American Silver*. New York: The Century Company, 1930.

Bigelow, Francis H. *Historic Silver of the Colonies and Its Makers*. New York: The MacMillan Company, 1917.

Buhler, Kathryn C. *American Silver*. New York: World Publishing Company, 1950.

Clarke, Hermann F. *John Coney, Silversmith*. Boston: Houghton Mifflin Company, 1932.

Currier, Ernest M. *Marks of Early American Silversmiths*. Portland, Maine: The Southworth-Anthoensen Press, 1938.

Ensko, Stephen G. C. *American Silversmiths and Their Marks* III. New York: Robert Ensko, Inc., 1948.

Phillips, John M. *American Silver*. New York: Chanticleer Press, 1949.

Wyler, Seymour. *The Book of Old Silver*. New York: Crown Publishing Company, 1937.

WOOD CARVING

Chamberlain, Samuel, *Salem Interiors*. New York: Hastings House, 1950.

Christensen, Erwin O. *Popular Art in the United States*. London: Penguin Books, 1948.

———. *The Index of American Design*. New York: The Macmillan Company, 1950.

———. *Early American Wood Carving*. New York: World Publishing Company, 1952.

Kimball, Fiske. *Mr. Samuel McIntire, Carver, the Architect of Salem*. Portland, Maine: The Southworth-Anthoensen Press, 1940.

Lichten, Frances. *Folk Art of Rural Pennsylvania*. New York: Charles Scribner's Sons, 1946.

Lipman, Jean. *American Folk Art in Wood, Metal and Stone*. New York: Pantheon, 1948.

Pinckney, Pauline A. *American Figureheads and Their Carvers*. New York: W. W. Norton & Company, 1940.

Index

A Collection of Psalm Tunes, 96
Affleck, Thomas, 20
Alden, John, 13-14
Alford, Alfred, 34
Alford, Arba, Jr., 34
American Cabinet Maker, 39
American Philosophical Society, 47
Arnold, Benedict, 119
Ash, Gilbert, 23
Astor, John Jacob, 25

Babbitt, Crossman and Co., 105
Badlam, Stephen, 23
Bagnall, Benjamin, 44
Barnum, P. T., 56
Barry, Sir Charles, 12
Bassett, Francis, 103
Batterson, James, 44
Bauman, August, 9
Beissel, Conrad, 133
Bellamy, John H., 5
Belleek, 86
Belter, John Henry, 36-38
Belter, Mrs. John Henry (Louise
    Springmeyer), 36
Bentley, Rev. William, 5
Bigger, Peacock, 112
Blacksmiths, 115-116, 118-119
Blaisdell, David, 49
Blanchard, Thomas, 3
Boardman, Oliver, 104
Boardman, Sherman, 104
Boardman, Thomas, 104
Boethius, 43
Boettger, Johann Friedrich, 80
Bolt and Grew, 109
Bonaparte, Napoleon, 29

Boone, Daniel, 116
Boston & Sandwich Glass Co., 64-71
Boston Gazette and Country Journal, 43
Boston Massacre, 96
Boston *News Letter*, 126
Boston Tea Party, 96
Bouslover, Thomas, 99
Bowdoin College, 17
Brass, 107, 109-111
Braziers, 107, 109-111
Britannia, 105
Brodnax, John, 94
Bromley, William, Jr., 86
Bronze, 100
Brown, Harry A., 87
Brownwell, George, 126
Budd, John, 31
Bulfinch, Charles, 7
Bullard, Charles, 51
Bumpsteed, Thomas, 101
Burch, Cornelius van der, 94
Burgoyne, General John, 23
Burnap, David, 53
Burns, Robert, 85
Burt, Benjamin, 93
Burt, John, 93
Burt, Samuel, 93
Burt, William, 93

*Cabinet-Maker and Upholsterer's
    Drawing Book, The*, 20
Cabinetmakers, 13-41
Cabinet Maker's Directory, The, 20
Callicut, William, 94
Carder, Frederick, 76
Carter, John, 110
Casey, Samuel, 94

Cathedral of St. John the Divine, 76
Centennial Exposition of 1876, 136
Chairs
    fancy, 31
    history of, 13-15
    Hitchcock, 31-36
    painted, 31
    Phyfe, 27-28
    rocking, 36
    upholstered, 15-16
    Windsor, 21-22
Chandlee family, 45, 111
Chapin, Aaron, 14
Charlemagne, 42
Charming Forge, 61, 62
Cheney, Benjamin, 49
Chessbrough, William, 116
Chests, 13
    Connecticut, 14, 53
    dower, 134
China, *see* porcelain
Chippendale, Thomas, 20
Cigar-store Indians, 7-8
Cincinnati Art Academy, 12
Cincinnati Art School, 12
Circus wagons, 8-9
Clark, Decius W., 83, 84
Clark, Herman, 55, 56
Clark, Thomas, 103
Clasen, Dirck, 81
Clockmakers, 42-58
Clocks, 42-58
    banjo, 51
    "blinking eye," 58
    brass movement, 47, 57
    definition of, 42
    Equation, 54
    Girandole, 53
    Gothic, 58
    lyre, 53
    OG (ogee), 57
    pillar and scroll, 56
    shelf, 49
    steeple, 50-51
    tall, 44, 49, 50
    tower, 44
    "wag-on-the-wall," 53
    wall, 50, 51, 55-58
    water, 12
    wooden movement, 55-56

Cogswell, John, 18
Coldwell, George, 103, 104
Collier, Richard, 113
Colt, Samuel, 10
Comer, John, 103
Committee of Safety, 97
Conestoga wagon, 109-110
Coney, John, 93, 95
Constitution, 98
Copley, John Singleton, 49
Copper, 111
Coppersmiths, 111-115
Corning Glass Works, 77-78
Cottey, Abel, 44
Courtney, Hercules, 23
Coxe, Dr. Daniel, 81
Coxon, Jonathan, 86, 87
Crehore, Charles, 51
Crewel, 130
Cristalleries de St. Louis, 68

Danforth, Henry J., 104
Danforth, Joseph, Jr., 104
Danforth, Sarah, 104
Danforth, Thomas I, 104
Danforth, Thomas II, 104
Danforth, Thomas III, 104
David, Jacques Louis, 26
Davis, William, 44
Declaration of Independence, 21
Dennis, Thomas, 16-17
D'Entrecolles, Pere, 79
De Rivoire, Appollos, 95
Directory, 27
Disbrowe, Nicholas, 14
Dixon, Jeremiah, 46
Dodge, Ezra, 47
Doolittle, Isaac, 47
Douglas, Stephen A., 129
Dreppard, Carl W., 53
Drinker, Edward, 81
Drinker, Philip, 81
Drowne, Shem, 112.
Duffield, Edward, 45
Dummer, Jeremiah, 93
Dunlap, John, 23
Dwight, Timothy, 93

"Easterlings," 88
Eastlake, Charles L., 39

Edgell, Simon, 103
Edward IV, King, 100
Electroplating, 106
Embroidery, 126
Engraving, 90
Ephrata Cloister, 133
Erie Canal, 29
Evans, Davis, 23

Fenton, Christopher W., 83-84
Figureheads, 5-7
Finley, Hugo, 30-31
Finley, John, 30-31
Fisher, Richard, 64
Folwell, John, 21, 23
Foster, Stephen, 127
Fraktur, 132-136
Franklin, Benjamin, 7, 36, 45, 47, 60, 95, 117
Frankl, Paul, 41
Frost, Edward S., 130
Frothingham, Benjamin, Jr., 24-25
Frothingham, Benjamin, Sr., 24
Fry, Henry H., 12
Fry, William H., 12
Fulton, Robert, 115
Furniture, 13-41

Gage, General Thomas, 24
Gaines, John, 14
Gates, John M., 76
Gaw, Gilbert, 22
Gazette of the United States, 25
General Time Corporation, 57
George III, King, 22
Gillingham, James, 21
Glass, 59-78
  ancient, 59
  art, 72-73, 76
  blown, 59, 69
  bottles, 62, 63, 74
  crystal, 78
  cup plates, 71
  cut, 72, 73-74
  enameled, 62
  flint, 64
  iridescent, 75, 76
  lacy, 69-71
  Mary Gregory, 68
  molded, 62, 69

pressed, 69
stained, 75
Glassmakers, 59-78
Gleason, Roswell, 105
Goddard, John, 19
Goddard-Townsend Co-operative, 18-20
Goldsmiths, 88
Gorgas family, 45
Gorgas, John, 45
Gorham, James, 94
Gostelowe, Jonathan, 21, 23
Graves, Richard, 103
Greatbach, Daniel, 83
Greeley, Horace, 84
Green, Samuel, 103
Gregory, Mary, 68
Grier, Dr. Robert S., 10-11, 12
Griswold, Ashbil, 105
Gunsmiths, 49, 111, 116

Hadley, Thomas, 39
Hairwork, 132
Haldans, William, 39
Hamlin, Samuel, 103, 104
Hancock, William, 86
Hanneman, Charles, 113
Harbeson, Benjamin, 115
Harland, Thomas, 53
Harvard College, 93, 96, 97
Hitchcock, Lambert, 31-36, 53
Hitchcock, Mrs. Lambert (Eunice Alford), 34
Hoadly, Silas, 55
Holden, John, 103
Hollingshead, William, 95
Horsewell, William, 103
Houghton, Arthur Amory, Jr., 76
Hourglasses, 42-43
Huber, Jacob, 60
Hull, John, 91, 93
Hunneman, Paul, 109
Hurd, Benjamin, 93
Hurd, Jacob, 93
Hurd, Nathaniel, 93-94
Huthwaite, James, 15

Illumination, 132
Independence Hall, 5, 22
Ingraham, Elias, 58
International Silver Company, 105

Ironworkers, 115-119
Ives, Joseph, 56

Jackson, Daniel, 109
Japanning, 124
Jarves, Demming, 64-71
Jefferson, Thomas, 21, 51
Jenks, Joseph, 93
Jerome, Chauncey, 56-57
John, King, 88
Jones, Gershom, 103

Kaolin, 80
Kentucky rifle, 116
Kidd, Captain, 15
Kierstede, Cornelius, 94
King, Daniel, 109
Krauss, Johann, 133
Kubla Khan, 79

Lafayette, Marquis de, 29
Lancaster, 5
L'Art Nouveau, 39
Latrobe, Benjamin H., 30-31, 39
Leighton, William, 71
Lenox, Incorporated, 86-87
Lenox, Walter Scott, 85-87
LeRoux family, 94
Leslie, Robert, 45
Libbey, Edward, 72-74
Libbey Glass Company, 73
Libbey, William, 72
Liberty Bell, 109
Lincoln, Abraham, 129
Locke, Joseph, 72
Longfellow, Henry W., 13
Louff, Charles, 9
Ludwig, Mary ("Molly Pitcher"), 11
Luster ware, 84-85
Lutz, Nicholas, 68-69
Macnair, Andrew, 109
Madison, President James, 31
Manning, William, 125
Mansfield, John, 91
Marsall, Benjamin, 123
Martyr's Mirror, The, 133
Maryland *Gazette*, 109
Mason, Charles, 46
Mason-Dixon Line, 46-47
Massachusetts Spy, 49

Matzen, Herman, 8
Mayflower, 13
M'Calmond, James, 113
McFadden, Sally, 130
McIntire, Samuel, 3-5, 22
McIntire, Samuel Field, 4
McIntire, Mrs. Samuel (Elizabeth
    Field), 3
Melchers, Julius T., 8
Metalworkers, 88-125
    brass, 107-111
    copper, 111-115
    gold, 88
    iron, 115-119
    pewter, 100-106
    silver, 88-99
    tin, 120-125
Miller, Abraham, 84-85
Miller, Andrew, 84
Morris, William, 39
Mount Vernon, 22
Mount Washington Glass Company, 73
Mullens, Priscilla, 13
Myers, Myer, 94

Needlecrafts, 126-130
Negro craftsmen, 118-119
New England Glass Bottle Company, 67
New England Glass Company, 64, 72
New England Glass Works, 69
New York Crystal Palace, 84
Norton, Captain John, 83, 84
Norton, Julius, 83

Orrerys, 46
Ott & Brewer, 86
Otto, Heinrich, 134
Owens, Michael J., 74

Paperweights, 68-69
Parian, 83
Paris Exposition of 1900, 76
Paris *Exposition Universelles*, 39
Partridge, Nehemiah, 123
Pass and Stow, 109
Passmore, Thomas, 123
Patchwork, 126-129
Patterson, Edward, 120-123
Patterson, William, 120-123
Peace medals, 95

Peale, Charles Willson, 49
Peck, Seth, 120
Pennsylvania *Chronicle*, 123
"Pennsylvania Dutch," 117, 133, 136
Pennsylvania *Gazette*, 21, 112
Penn, William, 17
Petit point, 130
Pewterers, 100-106
Philips Andover Academy, 96
Phyfe, Duncan, 25-30
Phyfe, James, 30
Phyfe, Lachlan, 28
Phyfe, Michael, 30
Phyfe, Mrs. Duncan (Rachel Lowzade), 25
Pike, George, 39
Pine-tree shilling, 93
Pitman, Benn, 12
Pitman, Sir Isaac, 12
Polo, Mareo, 79
Porcelain, 79-85
Porter, Edward, 55
Porter, Levi, 55
Portzeline, Francis, 134
Potichomania, 130
Pottery, 79-87
    "art," 85
    Bennington, 83-84
    definition of, 80
    earthenware, 80
    redware, 81
    sgraffito, 81
    slip-decorated, 81
    stoneware, 81
Potts, C., 83
Princeton University, 46
Providence *Gazette*, 113
Pyrography, 131

Quilting bees, 127
Quilts, 126-127

Raleigh, Sir Walter, 115
Randall, David W., 39
Randolph, Benjamin, 20-21, 39
Reed and Barton, 105
Revere Copper and Brass Incorporated, 98
Revere, Joseph Warren, 98
Revere, Paul, Jr., 98

Revere, Paul, Sr., 25, 50, 95-98, 109, 113, 123, 124
Richardson, Joseph, 95
Rittenhouse, David, 45-47
Ritterhuysen, William, 45
Robb, S. A., 7, 9
Robertson, John, 109
Robinson, Enoch, 69
Rogers, Asa, 99, 105
Rogers, Simeon, 99, 105
Rogers, William, 99, 105
Rose, Philip, 123
Ross, Daniel, 36
Ross, George, 113
Rugs, 129-130
Rush, William, 5

Samplers, 130
Sanderson cartel, 4
Sanderson, Robert, 91
Savery, William, 21, 36
Schaats, Bartholomew, 94
Schimmel, William, 11-12
Schnorr, John, 79
Schumaker, Daniel, 134
Scrimshaw, 10
Sessions Clock Company, 58
Sheffield plate, 99
Sherald, Josiah, 21
Sheraton, Thomas, 20
Shirley, Frederick, 73
Shop signs, 7
Shrimpton, Henry, 103
Silversmiths, 88-99
Skillin, James, Jr., 7
Skillin, James, Sr., 7
Skillin, John, 7
Skillin, Simeon, Jr., 7
Skillin, Simeon, Sr., 7
Sons of Liberty, 23, 96
Soumain, Simeon, 94
South Carolina *Gazette and General Advertiser*, 113
Sower, Christopher, 44
Standish, Captain Miles, 13
Steinman, Frederick, 113
Sterling silver, 89
Steuben Glass Works, 76
Stevens, Alfred, 123
Stevens, Samuel, 123

Stevens, Zachariah, 123
Stiegel, William Henry ("Baron Stiegel"), 60-63, 118-119
Stover, Richard, 93
Stoves
  cast iron, 117-118
  Franklin, 117
  soapstone, 117
Stowe, Harriet Beecher, 39
Sumner, William, 44
Sundials, 42-43
Sylvester II, Pope, 43
Syng, Daniel, 95
Syng, John, 95
Syng, Philip, Jr., 95
Syng, Philip, Sr., 95, 109

Taber, Elnathan, 52
Terry, Eli, Jr., 56
Terry, Eli, Sr., 53-56
Terry, Henry, 56
Terry, Mrs. Eli (Eunice Walker), 54
Terry, Samuel, 56
The White House, 31
Thomas, Aaron, 57
Thomas, Seth, Jr., 57
Thomas, Seth, Sr., 55, 56, 57
Tiffany, Louis Comfort, 74-76
Tinsmiths, 120-125
Toleware, 124-125
Touch marks, 100-101
Townsend, Christopher, 19
Townsend, James, 19
Townsend, Job, 19
Townsend, Peter, 119
Trask, Israel, 105
Trask, Oliver, 105
Tufft, Thomas, 21

United States Pottery Company, 83
University of Pennsylvania, 46, 47, 95
University of Virginia, 51

Vernon, Samuel, 94
Victoria, Queen, 12, 73
Vorschrift, 133

Wampum, 131
War Between the States, 11, 72, 85
War of 1812, 63
Ward and Couton's Furnace, 119
Washington, George, 5, 21, 22, 25, 60
Washington, Martha, 60
Waugh, Sidney, 76
Whitmore, Jacob, 104
Whittling, 9-10
Will, Colonel William, 103
Willard, Aaron, Jr., 53
Willard, Aaron, Sr., 52-53
Willard, Benjamin, Jr., 49-50
Willard, Benjamin, Sr., 49
Willard, Henry, 51
Willard, Simon, Jr., 52
Willard, Simon, Sr., 50-52, 58
Willet, Marius, 23
Willet's Pottery, 86
Williams, Otis, 104
Williams, Roger, 15, 43
Winslow, Edward, 93
Winslow, Kenlem, 13-14
Winthrop, John, 5
Wistar, Caspar, 59-60
Woodcarving, 3-12
World's Fair of 1893, 74
Worshipful Company of Pewterers, 100
Wright, Frank Lloyd, 41

Zion Lutheran Church, 62

SIGMUND A. LAVINE

has two ambitions—to own a talking parrot and to spend all his time digging out little-known facts about people and animals. As yet he has not acquired the parrot, but he has devoted long hours to the search for colorful material to enliven his biographies and nature books.

Neither a parrot nor research interested him as a young man, for he was determined to become an actor. This was only natural since his parents were members of John Craig's famous stock company. However, persuaded by stars, bit players, and stagehands to "get an education," he enrolled in Boston University's School of Journalism.

While in college he edited the campus humorous monthly, was feature editor of the weekly newspaper, played leads in Shakespeare productions, and stage-managed five annual presentations of the Gilbert and Sullivan Association. Out of this last-named activity came his hobby of collecting anything "by or about" the creators of *The Mikado, Pinafore,* and the other Savoy operettas.

Meanwhile, he became more and more active in newspaper work, both as a feature writer for the *Boston Sunday Post* and as sports correspondent for two wire services, but acting ambitions were not forgotten. Then came the Great Depression and, as there was no demand for either journalists or actors, he returned to the classroom.

After receiving his M.Ed., he taught in a United States Government Indian School at Belcourt, North Dakota, for two years, learned to speak both the Sioux and Cree languages, and talk in sign language. He was invited to tribal dances, ceremonies, and Indian court in reservations throughout Canada and the Northwest.

Upon returning to Boston in 1934, he began teaching in the schools of that city and is now an assistant principal. As soon as he became accustomed to the feel of concrete rather than prairie under his feet, he began to transcribe the field notes he had accumulated while observing wildlife in North Dakota, and he continued his study of scientific literature dealing with the ways of animals.

In time, out of this continuous research came nearly a dozen nature books. Meanwhile he was lecturing on Indian folklore and current books, writing natural history articles and literary criticism. He still engages in these activities and his work has appeared in national publications, while his column on books for young adults is a regular feature of the Boston *Herald*.

With his wife, their son Jerrold, and a whippet answering to the unlikely name of Morrisey—the latest of a long line of prize-winning dogs owned by the Lavines—he lives in a house filled with books, fish tanks, art glass, and historical china. For relaxation, his family attends country auctions, goes "antiquing," or browses in bookstores, but their greatest pleasure is truck gardening on a piece of rocky New Hampshire land.